MY LASTING MEMORIES

FELIX VARELA COLLECTION # 53

EDICIONES UNIVERSAL, Miami, Florida, 2014

HENRY PUJOL

MY LASTING MEMORIES

Copyright © 2014 by Henry Pujol

First Edition, 2014

EDICIONES UNIVERSAL
P.O. Box 450353 (Shenandoah Station)
Miami, FL 33245-0353. USA
Tel: (305) 642-3234 Fax: (305) 642-7978
e-mail: ediciones@ediciones.com
http://www.ediciones.com

Library of Congress Catalog Card No.: 2014953632
ISBN-10: 1-59388-264-5
ISBN-13: 978-1-59388-264-8

Typesetting: María Cristina Zarraluqui

Cover design: Luis García Fresquet

No part of this book
may be reproduced without
written permission of the author.
For information write to
Ediciones Universal.

To My Wife Katy for her love and patience

To my children Henry Luis and Mary Jean, my pride and joy

To my grandchildren, Allison, Michael, Caroline and Katie, my hope and aspiration for a better future

Table of contents

Prologue 9

Introduction 11

The Jesuits 15

El Esquivel 25

Mata 31

Sagua la Grande 35

Baldor 43

Pujol – Radelat 49

Life in the U.S. 59

New York City 73

My Professional Life 89

9-11-2001 113

Retirement 119

Prologue

This is not my autobiography. It is a compilation of my life's experiences and memories.

I have finally decided to write this book that I could leave behind for my children, grandchildren, and their descendants. After many months of thinking about it, I came to the conclusion that it was important to let them know how I have lived my life and how I have handled setbacks and disappointments.

To set the record straight, if I had to do it over again, I will do exactly the same thing with one exception. I will correct my mistakes before they happen —but then again, that is what life is all about— a series of experiences, good and bad that increases your wisdom and improves your resilience.

We spend most of our life learning so now I think it is time for me to share on a variety of subjects related to life, work, marriage and parenthood. Who knows, there may be some lessons learned that can still be applied.

I also want to thank my wife of 50 years, Katy Mata Pujol, who pushed me to write this book and who has given me more than I could had expected in a marriage. A loving wife, caring mother and adoring grandmother —a superb human being.

Introduction

It was December 31, 1958. The children were celebrating New Year's Eve, playing and throwing fire crackers into the air. All of a sudden, the news came on the radio that Fulgencio Batista, Cuba's strongman had fled the country and had left behind a military junta as a caretaker government. It was soon afterward that Fidel Castro and his band of rebels arrived in Havana and took over the government. I was 15 years old and had no idea what this change will mean for my family and myself. It was the beginning of a long transformation —my teenage years were about to change radically.

Cuba had a long history of democratic governments and dictatorships. It was the product of a country that was too close to the United States and never matured as a democracy on its own. It acquired its independence on May 20, 1902 after the Spanish American War and four years of the American occupation of the island. So, by all standards it was a young republic. It needed more time to mature but unfortunately it became part of the Cold War. The result was a devastating calamity for a prosperous people who only wanted to raise a family, educate their children and provide an opportunity for growth. The promise of free elections in 18 months and respect for the three branches of government soon disappeared and lies became the norm in the new government. The island became a big farm for the Castro brothers and its people the animals in that farm.

A year later, my father left for the United States and asked that we sell everything and start getting ready to move north. It was May 1960. My dad was an American citizen, born in Key West, Florida on July 4, 1908 —a date he was very proud of. So, by virtue of his American citizenship, both my sister and I were American citizens as well. But more about this later.

The big exodus was just starting —Communism was the new form of government. A dictatorship of the right was replaced with a dictatorship of the left, most brutal and inhumane that anything Cuba had experienced up to that moment. Businesses were confiscated; new reforms were established with the sole purpose of ultimate control by the government of all economic elements of society. No one escaped this new wheel that was trying to crush everything that Cubans had been used to and worked hard to maintain. A rebel army that promised to bring new democratic principles to the island, became a cruel and despotic army, led by Fidel Castro. It was the beginning of the end for a prosperous nation. Yes, there was poverty but also there was a good economic system that was improving every year. However, Fidel took that poverty and instead of improving it he just distributed all over the island. And, after 55 long years Cuba is in a dismal situation, not because of the embargo (since Cuba has relations and commerce with every other nation in the world) but because of their disastrous policies and their inhumane treatment of its people that has destroyed all motivation and aspirations of a productive and intelligent people.

One of the groups that were most affected by the new regime was the Catholic Church. Most of the priests and nuns were of Spanish origin. The government immediately started to take over those institutions, including Colegio Belen, one of the finest educational institutions in Cuba run by the Society of Jesus order (Jesuits).

The plight of the Cuban people began in 1959 and continues to this date!! Hopes and aspirations have been destroyed and all that remains is an impoverished island with a brutal and oppressive government.

The chapters that followed are my life's memories from all perspectives.

The Jesuits

The other day, as I was driving my grandson Michael to his middle school, he asked me if I went home for lunch when I was a kid in school. He is taking a Spanish class and the teacher asked him to find out. This question brought me back to my early days with the Jesuits. Memories that are still so vivid in my mind! The Colegio Sagrado Corazon de Jesus was a major landmark in my hometown of Sagua la Grande. It had a beautiful Gothic spire in the main church that you could see as soon as you cross the bridge over the Undoso River. The school building had an interior courtyard with the classrooms all around it. Behind the main building there was a huge field where all kinds of sports were played. There were

The church

a soccer and baseball fields as well as a handball and basketball courts. Lining the rear of these field were beautiful almond trees which were a delicious treat for us during the season.

The Jesuits had a distinctive influence on my character and behavior. St. Ignatius of Loyola founded this religious organization on August 15, 1534. Together with six of his friends he started a religious order that would focus on following on the footsteps of Jesus Christ. The Society of Jesus concentrates its efforts on four distinctive areas: missionary works, human rights, social justice and higher education. Cuba in the 50's had three Jesuit schools concentrated on higher education: Colegio Dolores in Santiago de Cuba, Colegio Sagrado Corazon de Jesus in Sagua la Grande and Colegio Belen in Havana. Colegio Belen was the most prestigious catholic institution in Cuba. Years later after the Castro revolution, Belen again started its mission in Miami, Florida where it is today considered one of the best catholic schools in South Florida.

I have very fond memories of my life with the Jesuits. They were formative years that provided me with discipline, organization, and love of country and love of Jesus. My maternal uncles all went to this same school. Classes were split into a morning and an afternoon session with time in between to go home for lunch. There was a well-known educator, Hermano (Brother) Parada who taught my uncles and me the basics of how to read and write. He would use metaphors like the noise of a machine gun to teach us how to read. For example if you use the sound of a machine gun together with the vowel "a" you would get "RA" and so on. It was a very ingenious way to teach young children the basics of reading. He also taught the 3rd grade class. I remember one time we were learning how to identify the different teeth in our anatomy class, Hermano Parada, in order to make his point clearer, proceeded to take a handkerchief from his pocket and then pulled his false teeth and showed us with a pencil the different teeth and their names. Every time I misbehaved he would compare me to one of my uncles who used to misbehave in the same way. So, I never heard a complement based on my uncles but only the bad things that I did. The Jesuits were strong disciplinarian and believed in corporal punishment as a way to control behavior. This was not unusual in those days. The belief was that kids would learn to behave better if they were physically punished with either a ruler or the slap of the hand. Of course, in today's standards that would be viewed as horrific punishment but we were used to and, as far as am concerned it did not have any emotional impact on any of us. You knew the punishment always so if you did something wrong, you would know the consequences. They taught a very important lesson: you have to learn to live with the consequences of your decisions, good or bad.

I remember one time as we were all falling in line right after the morning recess and one of the kids was "fooling around" and did not pay attention to the whistle which required that you get back in line. So, the priest in charge of this activity, Father Altamira, went over and slapped him. The kid try to return the punch and that was when all hell broke loose. Father Altamira gave him a good beating and from that day on he was one of the best behaved kids in our school! Another time when I was in 2nd grade, there was a student sitting behind me that used to bother me by tapping on the back of my chair so I got upset and when the priest, Father Sanchez, saw this he told us that we would settle this outside during recess. So, when recess came, he took us outside, made a ring with the other kids and told us to go ahead and start punching. This was new to me as I had never been in a fight before in my life but I remember my father telling me that if I was ever in a fight to start throwing punches right away, so that's what I did. Eventually, since I won the fight, the priest told us to shake hands and go back to the classroom. I never had any other problems with this kid or any other for that matter!

Hermano Parada
To my dear disciple, Henry. His teacher, Jose Parada SJ.

Our school was very traditional. You knew what to expect and one of the things we used to do is sing the St. Ignatius hymn. He was the founder of the Jesuit order.

Hymn to S. Ignatius of Loyola

Fundador sois Ignacio y general de la compañía real
que Jesús con su nombre distinguió
la legión de Loyola con fiel corazón
Sin temor enarbola la cruz por pendón
Lance, lance a la lid fiero luzbel
a sus monstruos en tropel.
Del luzbel las legiones se ven ya marchar
y sus negros pendones al sol enlutar
Companía de Jesús corre a la lid, a la lid.
Del infierno la gente no apague su ardor
que ilumina la frente de Ignacio, el valor
Ya voces escúchanse de trompas bélicas
y lanza sus lábaros en la batalla campal.
Fiel presagio, del auro bélico y de la paz
del auro y de la paz.

My first sport was football (soccer). Most of the priests were Spanish and very good at this sport. We were required to learn how to play this sport. At first you were afraid of the ball, especially when it was coming at you at about 100 mph so Brother Parada would chase you all over the field kicking the ball to you until you got rid of that fear. It worked!

I spent seven years with the Jesuits. Since I started first grade very young, my mother, at Hermano Parada's recommendation requested that I repeat that grade again to make sure I develop right reading and writing skills. I made very good friends at that school and after so many years we are still close and get together socially.

One of the areas that the Jesuits concentrated on was missionary work. Most of this work was done in Asia. Sometimes a missionary Jesuit priest would come to school and give us lectures in the church. He would always talk to us with his eyes closed and would relate his experiences of evangelizing in China. Just like St. Francis Xavier, he also dedicated his life to promote the life of Jesus in that part of the world.

The author – school picture

Once a year we would celebrate the Father Rector's (School Principal) birthday. On that day there was no class but calisthenics, fun and games in the schoolyard. We used to love that day, as we did not have to sit in class and do homework. Hermano Parada would go around handing out candies!

On weekends I would meet my friends and go to school to play baseball. Cuba had a professional winter baseball league with four teams: Habana (Lions), Cienfuegos (Elephants), Almendares (Scorpions), and Marianao (Tigers). If you lived in Sagua la Grande you were supposed to be a fan of the Almendares team only because their stellar pitcher, Conrado Marrero was from Sagua. And during the summer, we would keep tabs of the Major Leagues with the Yankees being the favorite team for the majority of Cubans. So, as avid baseball fans, we would play the sport trying to imitate one of the major league or winter league players. I used to play first base on those days so my idol was an American player that played for the Almendares team, Rocky Nelson who was also a first baseman so I would try to imitate his batting style. We had fun on those days!!

Sometime during those years I wanted to be more involved with the actual mass so I became an altar boy. This was a big thrill for me, as I had to learn the whole mass in Latin. In those days, prior to Vatican Council II, the whole mass was said in Latin and the altar boy had to respond to the priest instead of the congregation. I remember one time, I was assisting the priest on Friday evening masses and one of the duties of the altar boy was to ring the big bell just prior to mass. So, I got to school and put on my special vestments, As I started to pull on the rope to ring the bell, the sacristan came over to tell me that there was no mass that evening. I felt really bad and was hoping no parishioners had heard the bell and would come to church thinking there was a mass. I went outside of the church to try to alert them but, fortunately, no one showed up. I guess I was the only one who did not know there was no mass on that Friday. Another one of the duties of altar boys was to help make the wafers for Holy Communion. It was a technique very similar to making pancakes except that the mixture was lighter. You poured this mixture on an electric grill and wait for it to solidify. Then you would remove it and when it was cold we would use this special cutter that would make up the small wafers. The big benefit of helping out was that there was a lot of leftovers, which we would then eat, assisted with a little Spanish wine!

One of my favorite times with the Jesuits was Christmas. The Jesuits were famous for their Nativity set, which they displayed in their main reception area. When you saw it you felt you were transported to Bethlehem as everything looked so real. The shepherds, the three kings as well the terrain all looked so natural and real that people from town would come to see it. We would also have an end of the year party with a group of students participating in a play about the birth of Jesus and the choir singing Spanish carols. It was a beautiful time and also the end of school for the next two and half weeks. School would end just before Christmas and resume right after January 6, Epiphany Day. By the way, this was the day that every boy and girl in Cuba received his or her presents from the Three Kings (Magi).

School year normally ran from early September to early June. Many summers before going to the beach, my mother would send me to my aunt Berta's farm. She would put me on a train which would take me to Lugardita, the name of their farm, to spend a couple of weeks with my aunt Berta and uncle Lorenzo. This was much fun. I would get up very early, around 5am have a hearty breakfast and then join the men on our rides to move cattle from one area to another one. My horse's name was Estrella and this horse had a terrific trot. Estrella used to be the horse of Jose Ramon, my uncle Lorenzo's dad. During the afternoons my aunt used to make taffy which I loved. Their farm was very big. They owned a lot of cattle as well as sugar cane. I remembered wonderful times there and they were always very nice to me.

As soon as I return from the farm, we would leave for Varadero beach on the north coast of Cuba between my hometown and Havana. We used to spend a couple of months there together with my aunt Chela's (my mother's identical sister) family. Varadero Beach was well renowned for its white sand and beautiful water. Our parents would rent a house in the Dupont neighborhood of Varadero. The beach was beautiful with white sand and blue turquoise color water and our time there was very enjoyable from horseback riding to excursions to the other side of the beach as well as fishing. We had good friends and used to spend time fishing, playing games and riding horses. My cousin Ruly and I loved to go to the south side of the beach where there were a lot of rocks and caves. We used to think we were indians living in those caves. Fishing was also very good. My godparents, Luis Radelat and Clariza used to spend a week with us during the summer and he loved to fish. He used to say that in order to fish you had to have a lot of patience. I believed we went to Varadero beach for a couple of years and then came El Esquivel!

Over the last 15 years in our quest to find a beach that would resemble what we left behind in Cuba, we discovered Siesta Key, a beautiful beach on the west coast of Florida in Sarasota. We have been vacationing there with the whole family every summer and whenever we go, it brings back memories of El Esquivel, the beach that I used to spend summers with my family and cousins in Cuba.

El Esquivel

The most beautiful beach in Cuba was El Esquivel, at least to all of us Sagueros. My grandfather, Eduardo Radelat was one of the founders of this piece of paradise on the northern coast of Cuba, just 8 miles (13 kms) from Isabela de Sagua. Isabela de Sagua was a major shipping port for most of the sugar that was produced in the Sagua region. It had a deep channel where big container ships could come in, load up the sugar sacks and depart for many destinations across the U.S. El Esquivel was a private beach owned by the Sagua Yatch Club. In order to visit the beach and use its facilities you were required to be a member of the Club. The beach had two rows of homes stretching the length of approximately half a mile. There were two hotels: Hotel Morejon, closest to our house and Hotel Ortiz further east. I remember staying in the Hotel Ortiz one season before we built our own house. There was also a pier on the southern part of that key where pleasure and ferry boats carrying passenger would come in. During the week, there was one ferry boat, Dolores, that would make the trip twice a day – the first trip early in the morning, arriving at the key around 9am and then returning back to Isabela before noon and then another trip back to El Esquivel early afternoon and back to Isabela around 5pm. On Sundays, because of the volume of members that wanted to spend time at the beach, there were three ferries making that trip: Dolores, Kismet and Zorroza. It is important to note that these ferries were used during the sugar production seasons in the winter as pilot boats escorting the big container ships in and out of the port of Isabela de Sagua. Then during the dead season in the summer they were used to ferry passengers to El Esquivel.

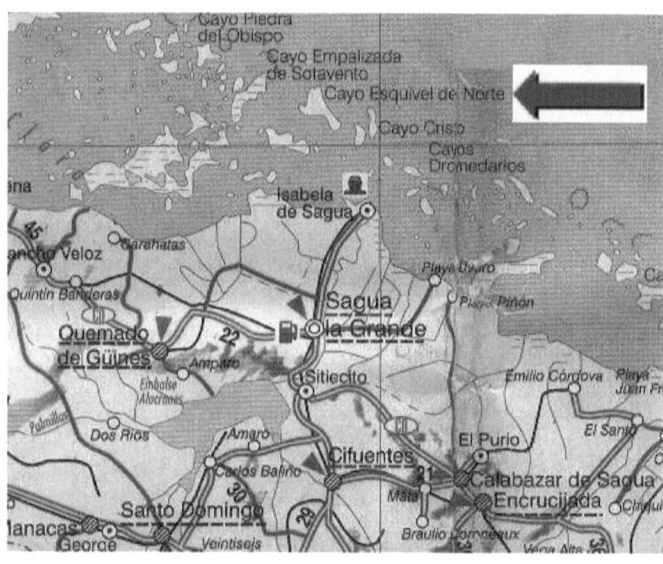

Our families used to go the El Esquivel right after school ended sometime in mid-June and would stay there permanently until early September. My mother and my aunt Chela's family shared the house, which we call caseta or bungalow. So, all the cousins were there together all summer long. My dad and my uncle Raul would visit occasionally since they had to work full time. Our caseta had a walk-around portico where we had lounge chairs ending with the big table where we had our meals. Inside were two large rooms on either side of the hallway. The right side was the Pujol family bedroom and on the left side the Oquendo family. Right after the bedroom there was a small space with a refrigerator on one side and a water filter on the other side as well as some closets. The last part of the house was the kitchen on the left and the bathrooms on the right. It was large enough for all of us with plenty of windows. Because of the potential for sand fleas during calm nights there was also a huge mosquito net that cover all of the beds on either side of the hallway. This was always used at night to make sure we would not be awaken to the bites of hundreds of sand fleas in the event of no wind.

In addition to our bungalow, there was also my grandfather Eduardo's with his wife and two daughters, our aunt Berta's (my mother's older sister) and her family, and my great aunt Maria Radelat's (my grandfather Eduardo's sister) and her family. So, my family had more relatives living on that beach all summer than any other family there. Needless to say, how difficult it was for us kids to do anything wrong as we were always being watched by some member of the family.

Our times in El Esquivel were completely carefree. We would get up around 7:30am, just before the ferry arrive and then have breakfast. After breakfast we would go and get together with our friends to play games while waiting to go in the water, something we could not do until 2 hours after breakfast in order not to have a bad digestion! So, around 11:00am or so we would all go into the water where we would stay until around 1pm. After that was a quick shower, lunch and rest. In the afternoon we would again go back in the water for another couple of hours. At night we would all gather in the hotel dining area where there was a jukebox and we would all dance rock and roll or cha cha cha. Sometimes we would go fishing or oyster collection by the mangroves. On some other times the adults on the beach would organize an excursion to Cayo Roteño in order to collect hicacos, a fruit similar to a prune that needed to be cooked by boiling and adding a lot of brown sugar. This regular excursion was exciting. It was long and we had to cross a lagoon, which during high tide, we would have to swim across. The younger children would be carried on the adults' shoulders. We also had to deal with the "diente perros" or jagged rocks along the edge of the water. But it was worth it. The Roteño beach was beautiful. While us kids would go swimming, the old folks were busy picking up the hicacos. Others collected shells of all kinds and colors.

El Esquivel had some basic infrastructure. For electricity, there was generator that used to be on from 6am until midnight. Just before midnight, the lights would blink twice announcing that the generator would be turned off soon. The water that was used to shower came from a big tank that sat behind the bungalow, which collected rainwater during the rainy season. This water was used also to cook and to drink after it was filtered on a special local vat that sat in the kitchen. The water that was used to flush the toilet came from the ground. If you dug a hole deep enough, that brackish water was not salted and it was used for that purpose only. Most casetas had a well with fresh water. Our refrigerator was a kerosene type. I remember in the early days before we had this refrigerator that what we had was an icebox. The ferry would deliver ice every morning upon arrival at the pier and this was used to keep basic things cool, so when the kerosene refrigerator came it was wonderful. Also, since there was no supermarket on the key, we used evaporated milk as our basic milk supply for breakfast. From time to time, we would order milk to be delivered by the ferry in the morning. But this was rare.

It was a very rudimentary life but very healthy as well. We would spend the day with just a pair of shorts and nothing else. We would eat a lot of seafood and were always on the move burning fat and calories constantly. We had a very good network of friends, which used to do everything together. Sometimes after the lights were out at midnight we would get together on a full moon night and go serenade different people on the beach. It was a lot of fun. Every once in a while we would build a camp fire and cook hot dogs and marshmallows. But we were always fishing.

Some days we would get up and see a "chinchorro" taking place. This was something the local fishermen used to do in order to collect a lot of fish quickly. They would drop a long net far out in the sea in front of the key and started dragging that net towards the beach. When they finally arrived at the shore there were a lot of different fishes, big and small. The adults would normally buy fish right there to cook later but us kids wanted the small sardines which they would let us have. We used these sardines later during our fishing expeditions.

The only big problem we had was when the winds died down. Then the sand fleas would come in with a vengeance. There was a person in charge of using a big smoke-spraying machine whenever the winds died down in order to keep the bites to a minimum. That is the reason all bedrooms had this huge mosquito net to protect us from those sand fleas in the event there was a windless situation during the night while we were sleeping. But most of the time there was a very healthy wind blowing across the key.

The last time I spent in El Esquivel was the summer of 1959. The big talk among my friends from Sagua at the beach was this 15th birthday party for Katy Mata. Since I had spent up to now my first three years of Bachillerato (high school) studying in Havana, I did not know Katy but have heard of her through my friends. All of my friends had been invited to her party and they asked me to come along. Of course, I was not about to crash this party since I was not invited. However, with a little bit of push from my young aunts, Jenny and Lourdes Radelat and the rest of my friends, I decided to take a chance and go. The party was on Saturday, September 12, 1959 in the small town of Mata about a half hour drive from Sagua. Even though I did not know Katy I was very familiar with the town of Mata.

I felt uneasy about doing this but, somehow, unbeknownst to me, God had other plans.

Mata

Mata was a small town in the northern coast of Las Villas province. Three sugar mills surrounded it. My grandfather Eduardo Radelat owned a guava processing plant in that town. Guava is a very common tropical fruit in Cuba. Very sweet with a high percentage of vitamin C and used to make marmalade, guava paste and guava shells.

So, because of that I used to travel to Mata with my grandfather on a regular basis but only knew the family that my grandfather was associated with in the guava plant. Most of the time we would spend it at the plant or across from it at the Water Plant of the town picking up peonies, a small black and red hard seed. One time, there were some robberies in the guayabera (guava plant) and my grandfather decided to bring his dog, Sultan, to guard the plant at night. Sultan was a mix between a German Shepherd and a Pointer dog. Very nice but very protective and if he did not know you, watch out! Needless to say, the robberies stopped.

The town was very small with three pharmacies, with the largest one owned by Dr. Carlos Mata Silva, Katy's father and a professor of Physics and Chemistry in the Institute of Secondary Education in Sagua. I remember Dr. Mata from the time I was taking my final exam to graduate from elementary school, as he was one of the professors giving those exams in the Jesuit school where I was studying. My grandfather knew Katy's grandfather, Dr. Carlos Mata Trujillo who, like my grandfather, had been a representative to Congress and was also the first medical doctor Mata ever had. Some historians claim that the town was named after him. The story goes that when Dr. Mata was a child he lived in that region since his father was the administrator of Conde More's properties. Conde More was a very wealthy Spaniard who owned many sugar mills and properties. So, later on after Dr. Mata graduated as a medical doctor, he and his wife, Lorenza Silva were traveling from Havana to Cifuentes, the town prior to Mata. During the stop in Cifuentes they were asleep and woke up at the next stop which was the small village which later became Mata. He passed away in 1957 and, unfortunately, I never had to chance to meet him.

The day of the party I joined with other friends and went to Mata. Of course, there was no issue when I arrived and introduced myself to Katy and others. They knew of my family and welcomed me. The moment I met Katy, I fell in love. It was a very interesting feeling as if I had known her for a long time and the person I had in my mind to one day marry. During the party I tried to dance with her as much as I could. I think one of my closest friends who was attracted to Katy was probably sorry he asked me to come! It was a great party attended by a lot of people and everyone had a great time. I think I got home around 3am and could not stop thinking about her.

The next day, I decided I was going to go back to Mata to see her so I called my grandfather to see if he was going there on a business trip. Luckily he was so I went back to Mata and rang her doorbell. I think she was very surprised to see me so soon but I also think she was happy by her facial expression. I continue my courtship for weeks until one day on December 19, 1959 she agreed to go steady with me. It was a time of uncertainty in Cuba with the government already starting to take control over many of the major industries so I did not know what was going to happen. But one thing I was very certain of that one day Katy and I would be married. It was only a matter of time. We spent time together in school, at parties and during my visits to her house all throughout the rest of 1959 and the first half of 1960, until my departure from Cuba on September 27, 1960. I told her that I would be coming back soon and that one day we would be married.

The author with his future wife, Katy Mata, outing in Manacas, Cuba

I loved spending time in Mata. Katy's parents were very nice to me and on Sundays I would go with them to Santa Clara, the capital of the province, which was about one hour from Mata. Katy's dad had favorite restaurants in Santa Clara that he liked to go to. So, after lunch at one of these restaurants, we would go to the movies. On the way back home he would normally stopped and buy some snacks to have later at their house. I would stay there until about 10:00pm when I would catch the bus going to Havana and stopping in Sagua.

Sagua la Grande

Leaving Cuba was traumatic to say the least and as I was flying out of Havana it brought me memories of my last 16 years in the island. Memories that were mixed with emotion as I was leaving Katy behind and all of my friends to start a new life in a new country where I did not know the language or the culture very well. As I reminisce about my life in Cuba I started to remember the El Infierno distillery and our house on Cespedes Street.

In 1943, my paternal grandfather, Raul Lesteiro Lopez, had just been made the Managing Director of Destileria "El Infierno" or El Alambique as we used to refer to this plant. It was one of the largest distilleries in the Americas but it was on the verge of bankruptcy. Lesteiro was my grandmother Cira's second husband. I never met my dad's father, Jose Pujol Guerra. He passed away before I was born, therefore, Raul Lesteiro was a grandfather figure to me. He was a very smart and astute businessman who worked very hard and became successful in the Cuban sugar industry. He arrived in Sagua la Grande in the year 1943 with my father, Henry and my uncles Charles and Frank. It was the start of a new and productive enterprise. It was during this period that my father met my mother, Olga Radelat and after a short engagement, were married on April 25, 1943. It was a very interesting wedding as both my mom and aunt Chela, who was my mother's identical twin, were married together. My maternal grandfather, Eduardo Radelat walked them both to the altar.

I was born on February 5, 1944 in Havana, Cuba although I spent my next 16 years in Sagua la Grande. They say you never forget were you were born and Sagua has a special place in my heart and my memories of those years are precious to me. It was a nice small town with approximately 30,000 people. It was surrounded by sugar mills, and with industries like the Destileria "El Infierno", the Fundicion (Steel Foundry) McFarland and many productive small businesses that gave the town a comfortable economic environment. It had three catholic churches — the Parroquia or Parish Church in the main square of town, the Apostolado, a girl's school with its own church and the Colegio Sagrado Corazon de Jesus, a church and elementary school run by the Jesuits and located right across the river.

Sagua la Grande is located on the north coast of Cuba, about 4 hours east of Havana. It has a very deep river, El Undoso, which crosses the city and is also blamed for many floodings during hurricane season. The river is navigable all the way to the port of Isabela de Sagua and on to the sea. Many barges navigated it during the sugar cane season. These barges were used to transport raw sugar to big container ships awaiting at Isabela. Also, many of the local citizens kept their small pleasure boats on the river. Everytime we went to school we had to cross the river as the Sagrado Corazon school was on the other side of town. Our parents never like us to go near the river so, since it was forbidden, we try to go every chance we got. We felt we could handle it without any problems.

Sagua la Grande, Las Villas, Cuba

I have very fond memories of my early years in Sagua. Our first house was on Cespedes Street, right above the Isla de Cuba clothing store. This was a very spacious apartment on the corner of Cespedes and Maceo streets. It was from here that I started attending the Sagrado Corazon school. I would go downstairs and wait for the school bus.

I still remember when my mother gave birth to my sister Olga, about 3 years after me. She was carried up the flight of stairs in a chair. During lunch, since there was no television, I would listen to the radio. My favorite episodes were "Los Tres Villalobos", a western, Tangañika (?), a huge gorilla, Tamacun, and Leonardo Moncada, another western. I would listen to these programs while eating my lunch or dinner. There was no television yet. Another distinctive memory I have of those years in this apartment was when my older cousins Frank and Raul Pujol would come over and play with me. This one time, the Three Kings had left me my first bicycle with training wheels, so they decided they would teach me how to ride this bike without training wheels. It was grand to be able to do that and go fast. I remember riding all around the block until I was an "expert."

The author's aunt and mother (left to right). Identical twins

A couple of years later years we moved to a small house in Colon Street close to the river. We lived in this house one or two years until my uncle Frank Pujol and family moved to Havana. We then moved to the house located on Cespedes No. 99, right across from the Police Station. This house was very big since it was the house where my grandparents stayed in when they visited Sagua. Periodically they would come and stay there for about two weeks.

Family picture. From left to right: The author, father, mother and sister

Every time my grandparents announced a visit, for me it was like a big party since they would always come with a lot of people in their big Cadillac limo. In addition to the two of them and the driver, they would also bring the nurse Mireya, my grandmother's assistant, Carmelina and once in a while a guest. I remember one time, they brought my dad's cousin Charles Pujol, also known as Caco. Caco was a Franciscan Missionary priest and one of the happiest people I have ever known. He was fantastic and we bonded very well. He gave a mass at the Apostolado Church and I was his altar boy. This was a big thrill for me. Much later in life he retired and was asked to be sent to the mountains of Nicaragua to help poor indians find a better life. He trained a group of children and brought them to Carnegie Hall in New York City for a benefit concert. With the money he raised he went back and built a church and school. He died years later and is buried there. He was indeed a blessed man!

From left to right: sister, mother, father and the author

On weekends I would go to the Jesuits to play baseball, my favorite sport. And on other times, I would go hunting with my maternal grandfather, Eduardo Radelat. He was an avid hunter and I loved those days when we would take his boat on the river and stop at one of the farms in the area to hunt for pigeons and Cornish hens. We would bring the hunting dogs along with Toby, a wonderful Pointer dog leading the way to the spot where the birds were hiding. We would bring our lunch and spend the whole day out in the country. It was great doing this.

I had a lot of affinity with my grandfather Eduardo. I admired his demeanor and what he represented. Since we lived in the same town, I was able to spend a lot of quality time with him. He would tell me stories about my mother, aunts and uncles when they were young. My mother Olga was one of six children that he had from his first marriage with my grandmother Luisa. I never knew my grandmother Luisa as she died before I was born. After her passing my grandfather remarried and had two daughters who became my youngest aunts. They were born after me, so in essence they were more like cousins than aunts. We were very close. My grandfather had a unique set of experiences that he shared with me. He was a custom officer, a congressman, and a banker. Even though he never attended college, he had the wisdom that you learn from experiences. His father died right after his graduation from high school. He was planning to study medicine at the University of Havana, but was unable to do so. His dad's passing made him the head of the family and he had no choice but to go to work to support his mother and younger siblings. Since he was the oldest this weight fell on him. However, this never held him back. He did what he had to do and did it well, becoming a prominent member of the Sagua la Grande business and social community. I spent a lot of quality time with my grandfather. He gave me a lot of good advice that has remained with me throughout my entire life.

Sometimes during weekends I would ride my bike to his house to play monopoly with my younger aunts. We were very close and to this date it has continued.

Baldor

Upon graduation from the Jesuits in 1956, I moved to Havana to attend Colegio Baldor a secular school where most of my cousins were attending. My paternal grandfather, Raul Lesteiro, used to pay for all the grandchildren's schooling. I remember when I was close to graduating from the Jesuits; I had to tell my grandfather where I wanted to do my high school work. So, one night while they were visiting us in Sagua, I told him that I wanted to go to Baldor. He said that I would have to go as an intern in the school and not stay with any of my families in Havana. He also told me that in that new school, away from home, I would be just a number instead of the "prince" in my own house and he was not sure I could handle that move. I told him I could and would, so everything was settled.

I started my high school education at the Baldor School in Havana. Its founder and principal was Dr. Aurelio Baldor, an eminent mathematician and author of one of the most used Algebra books in all of Latin America. Although Dr. Baldor came from a very catholic family, his school was secular and open to all students regardless of religion. It is important to note that Cuban education was modeled on the European model where the high school or bachillerato as we call it, was very intensive and provided its graduates with a strong background in either the sciences or the arts, depending on their future field of endeavor at the university.

Colegio (Academia) Baldor – Secondary Education Building, Vedado, La Habana, Cuba

Before the first day of school my mother brought me to Havana to pick my uniform and the rest of what I would need to live at the school and away from home. I was very excited. It was a new adventure with all new experiences, closer to my cousins in the capital in a reputable educational institution. Little did I know that once my mother left and I was by myself at the age of 12, that everything sunk in. I felt depressed. I missed my family and my home surroundings. I used to stay all night crying and would write letters to my mother to come and get me out of that place.

But, I stayed and soon enough began to make new friends. Became more accustomed to my new surroundings and no longer wrote sad letters. Given that the change was fairly drastic, my first set of examinations caught me by surprise at the level of difficulty and the need to study harder and differently. So, my first exams were a total failure. That brought my mother to Havana to find out what was happening. My father gave me a good talk about the need to get serious and start getting good grades if I ever wanted to be somebody in the future and not to have to depend on anyone. I think the combination of those discussions and my shame in having let my parents down, created a new commitment on my part and the next exams were exemplary. One subject in particular was Ancient and Medieval History. The professor after grading my paper gave me an F and called me to his office to tell me that he thought I had copied all the answers, which, of course I did not. The problem is that he could not believe that I had made such a gigantic turnaround. So, after giving me an oral exam he realized that I had studied, knew the material and deserved an A.

On weekends my godfather, Luis Radelat would pick me up and take me to his house for the weekend. Of course, I was required to bring my books to study on Saturdays. He would always tease me about what we were going to eat Friday night. Since those were the days prior to Vatican Council II, all catholic families were not allowed to eat meat on Fridays so we would have seafood. Now during the day on Fridays at the school cafeteria they always prepared a mixture of tuna and boiled potatoes all mashed together which I hated, so my godfather would start the trip to his house by telling me that my godmother was preparing a delicious dinner of tuna and potatoes. To my joy and satisfaction what she really had prepared was a delicious shrimp in tomato sauce over white rice and black beans – a real feast for someone who had not eaten well all week! Many Saturdays, my godfather Luis took me to see my paternal grandparents, Raul and Cira in Santos Suarez, a suburb of Havana. They had a beautiful 3 stories house in a corner. I was treated like royalty when I was there. I would first go with my grandfather Raul to his office in Havana. The office was in the Royal Bank of Canada building. Afterwards we would come home and have a delicious lunch. And, of course, my grandmother always gave me some money which came in very handy.

A year later, my aunt Chela and her husband, my uncle Raul Oquendo, bought a house in a new community called Reparto Fontanar, close to Havana Rancho Boyeros International airport, and I began to spend weekends with them and my cousin Ruly who was about my age. We would spend time on weekends together playing baseball, going to the movies and the like and it made my time in Havana much more enjoyable. On some occasions, my grandparents Raul and Cira would send the car to pick us up and take us to their house in Santos Suarez for lunch and then the driver would take us to the movies. I spent three years at Baldor where in 1960 upon the closure of the intern portion of the school I returned to Sagua la Grande to continue my high school education at the Institute Pre-Universitary of Sagua. I came with mixed emotions – first I missed my friends at Baldor but also I was back with my childhood friends from Sagua who were all attending the Institute. It was a new short beginning. It only lasted less than a year. That summer of 1960 we would be making plans to leave Cuba.

I was glad to be back in Sagua. One of the advantages to being home was the fact that I did not have to go through the pain of leaving the house to go back to Havana. Every time I went home for vacation and it was time to return to Havana, I would start getting sad. My mother used to tell me that if I ever had any thoughts that made me sad, to erase them from my mind. She certainly did that herself as I always remember my mom as a person that most of the time was laughing at things. Even when she spanked me after I had done something wrong, she would then laugh it off. The return to Sagua was providential. This was the time I met Katy Mata and my times at the Institute were happy and in love. My mother was very supportive of my upcoming relation with Katy. She knew I had fallen in love with someone special and I was very happy.

Pujol - Radelat

My mother was a unique human being. She was born in 1917 along with my aunt Chela. They were identical twins and were born in Sagua la Grande. Like most twins, they were very mischievous and love sports. During their teenage years they became excellent basketball players to the extent that they were part of the Cuban Olympic team that competed at the Pan American Olympic Games held in El Salvador in 1933(?), and they won the silver medal! They were very close and their children were close too. We used to spend Christmas holidays together and also summer vacations. We were all part of a big extended family where we were more brothers and sisters than cousins. My sister, Olga was close in age to our cousin Chely and I was close in age with my cousin Ruly. Later on our youngest cousin Any was born and she became the baby of the family. My mother used to tell us stories about her early childhood and the pranks they used to play to my uncle Miguel, her younger brother. She would tell us about their years at the Apostolado School. Since she and my aunt Chela were identical twins, they would try to fool the nuns whenever they were punished. They would take turns to do the punishments so this way neither one of the two would spend much time completing the punishment. The nuns never found out who was in detention! During her early teenage years, my grandparents would go to the Esquivel beach and spend time there during summers. She loved the beach and enjoyed the water very much. But the thing that I remember the most about her was her sense of humor. She would always have a smile on her face and believed that if you work hard, good things would come your way. She was the eternal optimist and this trait helped her during her long illness later on in life.

Celebrating my maternal grandfather's birthday at his house in Sagua la Grande

The Radelat lineage can be traced back to the 1600's. During a trip to New Orleans years later, I made contact with the American Radelats which my grandfather Eduardo used to mentioned in Cuba. We have a relative, Dr. Paul Radelat, who found a lot of information about the family. It seems that the first Radelat, named Marie had an illegitimate son, named Louis. There is also a Louis Radelat listed in the National Archives in Washington, DC who came to fight with Lafayette during the Revolutionary War of Independence.

Later on, two brothers, Adolphe and Jean Paul. along with their mother moved from Lorient, France to New Orleans and started a corn mill factory. A few years later, the older brother Adolphe and his mother moved to Cienfuegos, Cuba where there was a French population. There he met and married a French girl, Gabrielle Dudot and had many children, including my great grandfather, Eduardo Radelat Dudot.

I met the American Radelat family and they gave us a copy of a genealogy chart which I helped them complete with our names and our children's name.

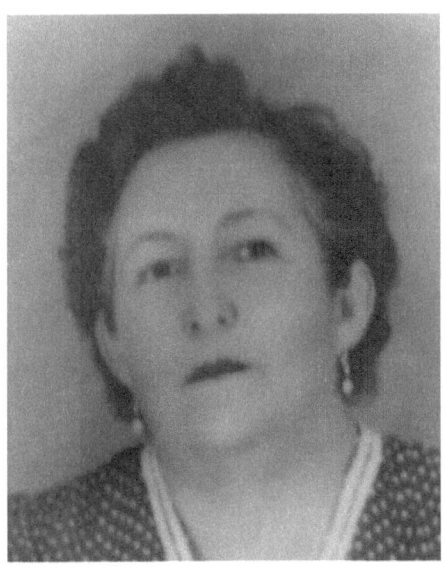

**My maternal grandmother
Luisa Olive Bravo**

In 1943 my father appeared on the scene in Sagua to work with my grandfather and uncles at the Distillery El Infierno. During a social dance at the Ladies Tennis Club they met and fell in love. At the same time my aunt Chela was also engaged to Raul Oquendo, a young mechanical engineer, recently graduated from Georgia Tech, who was working at the Fundicion McFarlane. So, they decided to get married on the same day and my grandfather Eduardo Radelat walked both of them down the aisle at the Parish Church in Sagua la Grande. It was a grand wedding something the town had never seen before or after. My father arrived in Sagua after having spent most of his life in the United States. He was born in Key West on July 4, 1908, the son of Cuban parents who had moved to Key West for business reasons. My dad would tell me stories about his early life in Key West and how him and his brothers were sent to St. Paul School, a Christian Brothers School in Covington, Louisiana. The only way to get there was to take the train from Key West to Miami since there were no roads linking the Florida Keys at that time. Henry Flagler built the railroad and you either took the train or a boat to Miami. Once in Miami they would change trains and travel to Covington. He did his elementary school there.

The author's father, Henry, in Sagua la Grande, late 40's

My dad was a very interesting person. He loved music including dancing and singing. After his elementary school years his family moved back to Havana where his parents were divorced. This was a traumatic experience for my dad. He was very fond of his father and loved him very much. His plan was to study Law at some point but all of that changed with the divorce. Soon thereafter my grandmother married Raul Lesteiro the "grandfather" I knew and things changed radically in my father's household. I do not have too many details of this period in my dad's life since he never used to talk about it. He would only say that his dad was a very smart businessman who spoke five languages. I do not know when he returned to the United States but what I know is that he lived there during the 1930's and return to Cuba just before WWII to work for his stepfather who was becoming a successful entrepreneur on its own rights. With my grandfather Raul's successful management of the Destileria El Infierno in Sagua la Grande, his fortunes changed and he became wealthy and powerful in the Sugar Industry. It was at this time that my father moved to Sagua where he lived until our departure for the U.S. in 1960.

The Pujol family started in Puerto Principe (now Camaguey) where my great grandfather emigrated to from Catalonia, Spain. He married Francisca Guerra Cisneros who was descendant from Salvador Cisneros Bentancourt (Marques de Santa Lucia), one of the Cuban patriots during the war against Spain. Cisneros Betancourt was president of Cuba in arms twice. His last role as President of Cuba in arms was to replace Jose Marti when he was mortally wounded in Dos Rios in 1895. We also had a relative, Benjamin Guerra who was Jose Marti's treasurer of the Cuban Revolutionary Party.

Benjamin Guerra committed suicide when he heard the news that Marti had been killed. He felt that everything was lost. My great grandparents had four children: Jose (my grandfather), Carlos, Mercedes and Caridad. My great grandfather, after the death of my great grandmother Francisca, and because of his political activities in favor of Cuban independence, was forced to emigrate to the U.S. and brought all his children with him. The two girls, Mercedes and Caridad, were enrolled at the Convent of the Sacred Heart in Albany, New York and the boys, Jose and Carlos were put in a military academy. Jose Marti dedicated a book to my great grandfather where he wrote: "To Jose Pujol Mayola poet in acts" and in other pages he referred to my great grandfather as "friend". Also, there is a story that Caridad was visiting Central Valley and they paid a visit and brought flowers to Jose Marti who was recuperating at the house of Tomas Estrada Palma, later the first president of the Cuban Republic. After the end of the war of independence, my great grandfather returned to Cuba where he was given a position in the first government of Cuba.

My paternal grandfather Jose Pujol Guerra

My paternal grandmother, Cira, and my Dad

My dad was an avid chess player. He used to train himself by playing alone using the Jose Capablanca chess methods. Capablanca was a world known Cuban chess player and champion. In addition to chess, his other hobbies were playing domino at the Liceo, a social club in Sagua, stamp collecting and other civic activities. He was very involved with the Odd Fellows and the Red Cross where he was captain of the regional office in Sagua. As a result of his work with the Red Cross we used to attend the stock car races that used to take place in the 1950's from Sagua to Havana. He had a very good heart and loved us very much. My father spent time teaching me baseball, how to build and fly kites and also bird catching. He would build the cages that we used to do that. He was very detailed on everything he did.

The author at his paternal grandparents' house in Santo Suarez, La Habana with his older cousins. From left to right, standing: Charles, Frank, Raul – seating: Cira and the author. All from the Pujol side of the family.

In May of 1960 my father told us he was going to Havana on a business trip. A couple of days later we received a phone call from him. He had left Cuba with my cousin Raul

Pujol and was in Palm Beach. Three months later we left Cuba as well. It was interesting to note that when my mother, my sister and I went to the airport to board the plane that would bring us to Miami, the custom officer told my mother that her children could not leave Cuba because they were Americans and needed a foreign card issued by the Ministry of the Interior. My godfather Luis Radelat told my mother not to worry and leave that he would take care of getting those cards and would send us the next day. This was great news to me since it gave another day to spend with Katy who had come to the airport with her mother to bid me goodbye. So the next day we went to the ministry with my godfather, got our foreign cards and left that afternoon to Miami. It was a short fly but full of emotions and expectations. Concern about our future, my parents' future and my relationship with Katy. But being the optimist that I am, I felt that it would not be long before I was with her again.

Life in the U.S.

I have always broken down my life into two basic periods: BC – before Castro and AC – after Castro. Most of what I have covered so far is the BC period. From my childhood, early school years, teenage years to our departure from Cuba to start a new life in a new country, my country by birth legally. I became an American Citizen the day I was born by virtue of my father being an American born in Key West. I never realized how important this would be one day and what responsibilities this would bring for me. At this time I had no idea what we were going to do in our new country. My main objective was to finish high school and then on to college. I was determined to be an electrical engineer one day and then marry Katy. Simple words with many actual difficulties involved. As far as my parents were involved I was not too worry since my grandfather, Raul Lesteiro was in New York City and we felt he would help my dad start a new life in the U.S.

Interesting enough, my grandfather gave each of the children an opportunity to either buy a business or receive a "pension" every month. This pension of course was small so getting into a new business made more sense. My dad decided to go with the business option.

During the period of May 1960 to September 1960, my dad met a gentleman from Tampa who owned a dry cleaning and shoe repair store in Ft. Lauderdale, Florida. The store was for sale and since my dad had worked in this business during his years in NYC, he decided to buy it. The name of the store was White Star Cleaners and was located in a very good commercial area in Ft. Lauderdale; right next door to the Sears Town on Federal Highway. Our store was next door to Allen Business Machine and two doors away from the Royal Castle in the corner. So, when we arrive from Cuba in September the store was already running under "new management". It had a shoe repair person named Jimmy, an elderly Italian man, a seamstress named Rose and an African American gentleman who used to come in the afternoon to iron all the dry cleaning clothes. In addition we had a pick up station in Davie. We felt that this business would be good to start our new life in the U.S. Unfortunately, my dad bought a business during the times of polyester in an area where most people wore shorts and tennis shoes. Not very promising!

The day after I arrived in the United States I started school at Ft. Lauderdale High, the "Flying L's". This was a very traumatic experience. A new school, just 2 days after I had left Cuba, a new language which I was not familiar with enough to carry on a conversation or understand the class lectures, new kids with different backgrounds and culture and a completely different educational style. The first day I sat in class I thought the whole world was on top of me. When I got home that afternoon I cried hard and felt very sad. My mother in her usual way talked to me and told me examples of people that had very difficult beginnings but that they never gave up. She told me that if I wanted to marry Katy one day I needed to become a professional so I could support my family and be "somebody". She said to be optimistic and work hard and that things will be better with time. So, that discussion with her helped me a lot and I decided to move forward and to not feel sorry about myself any longer. I needed to get serious, study hard and learn the language as quickly as possible. Everyone at school was very helpful and I started to make friends. There were only three students from Cuba in the whole school including myself. Since I had all the science courses from Cuba I enrolled in American Government, American History, English (Senior and Sophomore) and Typing. I had enough courses in Mathematics, Physics and Chemistry that I did not need to take those classes.

One day the guidance counselor called me to the office to introduce me to this kid named Peter. Peter was also a senior and his maternal grandfather was Chilean so every summer Peter would spend time with his grandfather in Chile but had a lot of difficulty conversing with him since his grandfather did not speak English at all. So, the guidance counselor said to us: Henry you need to learn English and Peter you need to learn Spanish so starting today you guys are going to become real close friends – Henry will speak to Peter in Spanish and Peter will speak to Henry in English. This way we would both benefit and learn the languages. This worked very well and eventually I started to grasp the language and was able to improve my overall school work and understand the new culture so much better. Peter eventually went back to Chile for the summer of 1961 with a better understanding of Spanish and I am sure he did very well with his grandfather. It was a "win-win" situation!

One of the courses I had the most difficulty with was American History. In Cuba we never learned American history in detail so I basically had to learn it from scratch in order to do well in the tests. I remember spending late nights translating from English to Spanish so I could understand all historical facts and in due time things started to get better. In fact, by the time I went back to Cuba during the Christmas of 1960 I already had a good command of the language. Yes, I went back to Cuba that Christmas to see Katy. But how was I going to pay for the flight and expenses?

Every day my father used to give me a fifty-cent coin to buy lunch in the school cafeteria. And every day I would save that coin and go through lunch without eating. Instead I used to walk to one of the streets near Las Olas Blvd. in Ft. Lauderdale and read my textbooks. I felt that if I stayed in school during lunch hour I would break my will power and spend the money. In time I saved a lot of money and when time came to buy a ticket I told my mother that I was planning to spend Christmas in Cuba. She was alarmed and curious as to how I was going to pay for the trip since we were a bit strapped for money. So, I showed her all the money I had saved. My dad then decided to help me with the rest and I bought a round trip ticket to Havana on Aerovias Q – a Cuban airline that used to fly from Ft. Lauderdale to Havana.

The time in Cuba during the 1960-1961 Christmas season was very challenging. I was happy to see Katy again but concerned with the situation in Cuba. There was already talk about an invasion and the political situation between the United States and the Cuban government was deteriorating daily. When I landed at the airport in Havana, Katy and her mom and my godparents were waiting for me. Havana was still beautiful and decorated with the Christmas ornaments as in the past. I traveled to Sagua with Katy's parents after spending Christmas Eve at her maternal grandparents' house in Cojimar, a resort town across the Havana Bay on the northern coast just west of Havana. In Sagua, I decided to stay at my grandfather Eduardo's house. One of my uncles in Sagua let me borrow one of their cars, which I used to travel to Mata on a daily basis to spend time with Katy. I brought my grandfather a shirt for a Christmas present and he was happy. However, bad things were looming on the horizon and on January 4, 1961 while I was in Havana waiting to board the Aerovias Q flight back to Ft. Lauderdale, the United States government broke diplomatic relations with the Castro government. This was the beginning of the embargo of Cuba.

During those days in Mata I told Katy that the invasion was coming and that soon we would all be back. Little did I know then that the Castro regime would remain in power for the rest of my adult life! Yes, the invasion came but did nothing to shake the communist regime. It was a total disaster with the advent of a new American President, John F. Kennedy and his inexperienced administration. Those Cubans that went on the invasion force were basically double crossed by the new Administration in Washington. There was no air support as promised. There was no naval support as promised and the invasion plans were basically changed guaranteeing a total defeat. The United States had an opportunity to get rid of an evil dictator but decided against it and we are still paying for it to this date. The British government told the new administration that the whole world would know the U.S. government was behind the invasion plans so the least they could do was win! But history repeats itself – how many times have our governments embark in wars without the total commitment to win? Wars, if fought should be won or the results would be worse than before.

After I return from my short Cuban holiday with Katy and family, I started school again. When I return I was starting to nurse a bad cold, which later turned into bronchial asthma. I used to have asthma as a young child and I suffer with it every time I caught a cold. So, this time was no different. I had to stay home for about a week and was able to watch the inauguration of John F. Kennedy on January 20. It was a very cold day in Washington but the President's speech was outstanding. It gave the whole world optimism that the U.S. would not allow communism to expand in this hemisphere. We all felt happy and optimistic that we would soon return to Cuba. And as we all know the April 1961 Bay of Pigs invasion was a disaster! It basically made Castro into a hero. He was able to battle the United States and win. This was the product of a young and inexperienced president more concerned about what the world would say than eliminating a brutal dictatorship 90 miles from the U.S. shores.

Early on in January, my aunt and uncle Raul and Chela decided to move to San Jose, Costa Rica to start a new life in the sugar industry there. My cousin Ruly was at the time a senior at Miami Senior High School and because of his parents' move he came to live with us in Ft. Lauderdale and transfer his credits to Ft. Lauderdale High. We were together again and both finished there, graduating in June 1961.

We lived in Ft. Lauderdale from September 1960 until May of 1962. I spent my time studying to complete my high school education and writing letters to Katy, every single day. But because of the delays in Cuba she would go sometimes weeks without getting any of my letters and then one day she would receive a few of them together. This was our way of keeping in touch. I was very hopeful that when the "invasion" happened the whole situation in Cuba would be resolved, we would go back and Katy and I would be together again. God had other plans.

The dry cleaning business was not very good and did not yield any significant profits. As a result of this both my mother and father had to get a job. My dad took a job working in the computer section at the First National City Bank in Miami on the night shift. My mother ended up working at a laundromat place washing dirty clothes for people who contracted that service. These were hard times but I never lost sight of my goals throughout this period of my time: Married Katy and get a college education.

The school year went on. I remembered studying for something called College Entrance Exam or SAT and doing poorly. I think the combination of my problems with English as well as the lack of understanding about this type of examination did not help me in getting a good score. However, I persisted in my quest to get into a college. Not knowing what it would cost, I applied, along with my cousin Ruly to Georgia Tech. His father, my uncle Raul, was an alumnus of Georgia Tech. My cousin was accepted but I was asked to come during the summer to make up some courses due to my SAT scores. After I reviewed how much it would cost and the fact that my parents did not have the money to pay for it, I decided not to pursue this any longer. So, in June 1961 we both graduated from Ft. Lauderdale High School. My cousin went on to Georgia Tech and I enrolled at Dade

County Junior College and started my first year in college. The costs were very reasonable and I drove to the school in North Miami every day.

Since I needed a car for my daily trip to Miami, my dad bought a used Fiat coupe, aqua color. It was semi-automatic and it was real cute. However, mechanically it was very unreliable. I remember one night as I was driving down to Miami to take an exam, the car broke down. I missed the exam and had the car towed away. But since I did not have the money to upgrade to a better car, I had it fixed and kept using it for the remainder of that school year.

One day, we received a call from Katy in Cuba to let me know that she was in the process of leaving the island for the U.S. I was very happy and when I told my mother she said that Katy could stay with us. Of course, her parents had another plan. They felt that the best thing for her was to go to New York City and live with her aunt Lucy, who did not have any children and had the financial means to take care of her. At that moment I started to think about moving to New York City. But how and when?

Katy arrived in Miami in January 1962. It was a very happy day for us. We had not seen each other since my short Christmas time in Cuba in December of 1960. She was going to stay with her cousin in Miami for a few days before departing to New York to begin her new life in this country. At the time I was in the United States Naval Reserve in order to fulfill my military obligations. I knew that the coming summer I was supposed to go to the U.S. Navy Great Lakes training center to do my boot camp training. So, I started to think about a trip to New York right after that. I had a lot in my plate: finishing my first year at Dade County Junior College, doing my naval training every week, and planning a trip to New York while helping my parents out at the dry cleaning store every day after school. It was a busy time but full of hope and aspirations. I had grown up fast. My teenage years had disappeared very quickly and I knew I had to mature and face my new challenges as best as I could in order to meet my goals in life. I never doubted what I wanted to be in the future and I think this is what kept me focused throughout this time.

One day during one of my many trips to Miami I went to see Katy's uncle to say hello. I was surprised to know that he needed to travel to New York with some friends from his days as a senator in Cuba but they did not have a car. He asked me if I would mind asking my father to borrow his car for the trip and since I would do anything to go to New York to see her, I promptly asked my father who agreed. I also asked one of my good friends from Cuba if he wanted to come and see the big city and he agreed. So, we all left on my dad's Peugeot station wagon and drove non-stop to New York. We all took turns driving and finally made it to the big city. We had reserved a room at a small hotel in Union City, N.J. As soon as we arrive, my friend Eduardo Torres and I left in my father's car to visit Katy in Manhattan.

We arrived at her aunt Lucy's apartment around 8pm, very tired and sleepy. My hope was to see her and then make plans for the next day to see the city highlights, etc. We rang the bell at her aunt's apartment in Chelsea and Lucy opened the door with a big grin to let me know that Katy was in Boston with some friends. Since I had not called (I wanted to surprise her) she had left a day before. However, Lucy immediately said that Boston was not far and that we could leave right away to go and pick her up. I assumed that she knew how to get to Boston since she sounded so sure about how far Boston was. Unfortunately she did not. Every time we reached a tollbooth on the turnpike she asked me to check with the attendant how to get to Boston. So, all in all, we reached Boston around 5:30am the next day. We phoned the house where she was staying and picked her up. We stopped at a restaurant for breakfast and headed back to New York. This time I asked my friend Eduardo to drive, as I was extremely tired. I sat in the back sit with Katy and as much as I wanted to talk to her, my eyes would continually close on me. I think I slept half the trip back.

We arrived in New York around 3pm and dropped them at the apartment. Katy's aunt asked us to come back later for dinner and then to go out and see the sights of Manhattan. We drove through the Lincoln Tunnel and could not find the motel that we were staying in. We drove for a while and finally got there. The first thing we did was try to get some sleep which we did for about 2 hours and then shower and return back to her apartment for dinner.

After dinner we drove around Manhattan looking at the major sights – St. Patrick's Cathedral, the Empire State Building, Times Square, etc. Again, I assumed that Katy's aunt who had lived there for a number of years knew how to get to all those places. So, when we try to find the Empire State Building she asked me to check with a patrol car that was parked near us. I asked the cop how to get to all the places I wanted to go and that is how we found the key attraction sights of New York City. The reason Lucy was unable to tell us how to find the sights was because she was used to taking the subway and was unfamiliar with streets name!

When we got to the Empire State Building, we parked the car and walk towards the building. I never forget my friend Eduardo's reaction when he looked up towards the top of the building and said: Boy, I thought it was going to be taller than this!!

So, later that night we left them at their apartment and returned to our motel. We slept fast and got up early the next morning for our non-stop return trip back to Miami. It was a very short trip!

In June 1962 I left with the rest of my naval reserve company to the Great Lakes Training Center in Waukegan, Illinois, about one hour north of Chicago. We flew out of Miami on National Airlines. I had mixed feelings about this but also excited. We arrived in Chicago in the evening and it was cool. Early June Chicago is a lot colder than Miami. We boarded a train to the training station. As soon as we arrive there was a Chief Petty Officer yelling out orders to get out of the train and to form a line into the bus. From the train station we drove to the Great Lakes Naval Training Center – a city in itself with over 30,000 sailors receiving training – both reservists as well as regular Navy. We went into this huge old building that look like a gigantic cavern where we were given our uniforms, barrack assignments and where we met the man in charge of our destiny for the next two weeks, Chief Petty Officer Stiles. There were 90 sailors in my company.

The training was intense. We had physical exercise periods during the day along with class training. We would wake up around 5am every morning and since I was in the barracks detail team, I had to go to the mess hall (cafeteria) for breakfast earlier than most other sailors. We would then come back to get the barracks ready for its daily inspection. We would check the cleanliness of the floors, lockers and bathrooms. Also the way the cots were neatly done. If we fail inspection, the whole company would have to endure long exercise periods, especially push-ups. One time I remember the Chief Petty Officer was coming around with a captain and they stopped at my locker and, it looks like they were impressed the way I had it organized. The two lockers next to mine were very messy so they got angry and threw them on the floor and told the sailors to get them fixed to look like mine. I did not gain a friend that day!

My two weeks at the Training Center went fast. I was looking forward to returning home and tell my parents everything that I had gone through and also to see if I could convince my dad to drive to New York City to see Katy.

Upon my return from basic training I told my dad I wanted to drive to New York City to see Katy. My dad thought about it and agreed. He had friends and cousins there that he had not seen in a long time and thought the trip would enable him to do so and also to check for job opportunities in the city. Since the dry cleaning business was not doing so good he felt that perhaps he could find something better in New York. The last time my dad had been in the city was during his mom's funeral.

My grandparents owned a beautiful apartment on Central Park South overlooking Central Park and a block away from The Plaza Hotel. They had bought that apartment in

1953 from the widow of the owner of Woolworth's 5 and 10 stores. The name of the building was the Hampshire House. They stayed there every time they came to New York from Cuba on business. During those trips my older cousins used to come and had a great time. There was always a big Cadillac limo parked downstairs for their use. In December 1958 when my grandparents left Cuba for the last time, they stayed at their apartment in the city. My grandmother started to miss her children so my grandfather asked each of the children to take turns traveling to the city and to bring one grandchild with them. Since I was already in high school in Havana, my sister was selected to accompany my father on this visit. My grandmother's health continues to deteriorate and finally in February of 1962 she passed away. This was very traumatic for everyone especially for my grandfather who was very distraught. Her viewing was at the Frank E. Campbell funeral home in Madison Avenue and was interred at Hartley Cemetery in upstate New York. Soon afterwards my grandfather sold the apartment and moved to Madrid, Spain where he died a few months later of a massive heart attack. This was the end of an era since so much of my family revolved around my paternal grandparents.

After their death and since there was no official will for the inheritance, the family hired an attorney who found out that one of my grandfather's secretary had forged the signature and was able to withdraw a very large sum of money from the Royal Bank of Canada and fled to Brazil where there are no extraditions laws with the United States. The family immediately sued the bank through the State of New York. The laws are such that in order to sue a banking institution you must do it through the state. We won the case and then had to prove to the State of New York that we were the legal heirs of the Estate of Raul Lesteiro. In order to prove our case certain documents had to be brought from Cuba. The Cuban government denied our requests and the State of New York kept our money. It was a sum of money in the millions of dollars!! This is one of the reasons I do not believe in inheritances. I believe that an inheritance should be given while you are alive but the best inheritance you can give your children is to provide them with a good education that they can later use to forge a successful future, the example of a life well-lived and the support they need along the way. My father who passed away in 1967 never saw the results of this lawsuit.

New York City

So, in May of 1962 my dad and I left for New York City. This was going to be a one-week trip. We made one stop on the way there and finally arrived in the city and went straight to Katy's apartment. Her apartment was on 21st Street between 7th and 8th Avenues. We made reservations at the Chelsea Hotel that was located on 23rd Street just a couple of blocks from their apartment. It was an older hotel but with class. This time I was able to see the sights in full and also got to ride in the Staten Island Ferry where you can see the skyline of Manhattan in its splendor, especially at night. We spent a lot of quality time together while my dad was visiting friends and relatives in the city.

One of the cousins my dad had not seen in a long time was Carolina Segrera Pujol. Carolina was the daughter of one of my dad's aunts. She was a professional soprano singer who had sung at the Scala de Milan earlier in her career. Now she had a singing academy in Manhattan. She was very happy to see my dad and they talked for a long time reminiscing about their childhood, etc. My dad also tried to find job opportunities but to no avail. He felt that he needed to move to New York in order to find a position worthy of his knowledge so this part of the trip failed.

Finally the week came to an end and it was time for us to leave New York. The eve of our departure, we again took the ferry to Staten Island and I told Katy then that I was planning to move to New York as soon as I could get everything resolved in Florida and that I thought my parents would probably follow me later. Of course, I had not told my parents any of my plans yet. I would talk to my mother first and get her advice. During our return trip I sent a letter to my cousin Raul Pujol who had an apartment in the upper East Side to ask him if it would be alright for me to stay with him until I could get a job and be on my own. I called him on the phone later and he agreed. So, now the only thing left to do was to ask my parents.

My mother, as usual, supported my decision and after discussing it with my dad, I made preparations to move from Ft. Lauderdale to New York City. This was exciting as it was the first time I was making a decision on my own. A decision that I thought was very beneficial for Katy and I as well as my parents, if they chose to join me later. The dry cleaning business was doing poorly so I felt that a change would offer my parents a better life in an exciting city like New York with more opportunities than in Florida. So, on a nice May morning I loaded my Chevrolet Corvair with my personal belongings and waved good bye to my parents and left for my big adventure. The trip was uneventful and after driving all day and into the night I finally decided to stop at a small motel in South Carolina. I do not remember how much it was but I had to pay cash and sign a large book with my name and address. The old man that was in this small office looked surprise to see such a young person, by himself, checking into a motel at such a late hour. After securing the room the best I could, I went to sleep. Frankly I was very nervous and don't think I slept very well so early in the morning I showered, got dressed and hit the road again, stopping soon for breakfast. In order to keep busy, I had the radio on. I remember that the popular hits of those days were Ray Charles' Georgia and Bobby Vinton "Roses are Red, Violets are Blue." One of the areas that I stopped was the South of the Border center just at the border of South and North Carolina. It was a much smaller place then than it is now but nevertheless full of trinkets and other items. I think I bought a small blade. I was always fascinated with blades since I was a little kid and thought this might come handy at some point.

The trip became very boring. I did not have anyone to talk to. I kept my mind focused on the reason why I was moving to New York. I started to create different plans in my mind. First I would want to enroll in a university, get a job and find a place to live. I was not sure my parents would come later. But as long as I was near Katy nothing else mattered. So, finally, around 9:00pm I crossed the Lincoln tunnel and I was in New York City. I drove to Katy's apartment where she lived with her aunt and uncle.

That night I stayed with them but the next day I rented a unit not far from their building which turned out to be a lovers' place. That night while I was trying to sleep, I kept hearing sounds coming from the unit next door. So, very quickly the next day I called my cousin Raul Pujol and he graciously told me to come live with him for as long as I wanted to.

That same week, Katy and I went to an employment agency. I needed a job fast in order to support myself. The agency sent me first to an office on the Hudson River that would handle different shipping containers on major liners. The job was from 4pm to 11pm and the pay was good. Unfortunately it interfered with my college plans so I turned it down. Next the agency sent me to Grolier Enterprises on Lexington and 52nd St. They were looking for a typist and I was a pretty good typist so I eventually got the job. It was very interesting since the office was primarily made of women typist with one exception, a gay fellow who was really very helpful to me. So, I started my first job in the big city making $55.00 a week.

The next mission was to enroll at The City College to continue my engineering studies. I wanted to be an electrical engineer and City was the best option. The City College had very stringent academic requirements in order to be admitted with a free tuition. I first started in the evening session and had to improve my grades before I could enroll in their free tuition program. So I studied hard and eventually was admitted as a free tuition student in their Evening Division program.

The Evening Division only allowed me to enroll on a couple of courses since I was also working during the day. So basically I would take around 6 credits a semester. Considering that I would need 169 credits to graduate it would take a very long time to finish. But, it did not matter at the time. I knew that at some point I would find a way to enroll in the Day Division and finish earlier.

Working life at Grolier was very interesting. Grolier was a book publishing company. Their most popular books were yearbooks to go with people who owned The Book of Knowledge and/or Encyclopedia Americana. These yearbooks were issued to update those two encyclopedias. My job was to read letters sent by customers and then decide based on the complaint what type of form letter to use. Most of the complaints were associated with customers not receiving their yearbooks or change of address. We had a form letter for every type of issue and my job was to type their name and address on each envelope and mail it. It was basic but so was the pay!

One day I received a call from my mom letting me know that they had sold their dry cleaning business and were moving to New York. I was very happy and imagine my cousin Raul was too since his apartment was very small for the two of us but he never complained. I will always be thankful for his generosity during the time I needed it most.

My parents and my sister arrived in Manhattan and booked a room at the Chelsea Hotel on 23rd Street. The Chelsea was an old hotel but with a lot of history. Many famous writers had stayed there. My parents had two basic missions: find an apartment and a job for my father. My father had lived in New York City when he was a young man and knew the city fairly well. He also had friends from Cuba who had settled in the city and he started to meet them.

One day, while riding a bus in Jackson Heights, Queens, at a bus station on Roosevelt Avenue and 81st St., under the elevator, my mom looked at the people in the sidewalks and saw her cousins Olive. They immediately got off the bus and met them. Everyone was surprised and happy. This was the beginning of our life in Queens. My mom's cousins all had apartments at the Alameda Apartment complex on 79th Street and Roosevelt Avenue, just behind Elmhurst City Hospital. They immediately went to the building to meet the superintendent to rent a unit. There was a unit available on the second floor of the C section. This building had three sections – A, B, and C. The apartment they rented was C202. My father went with my mom's cousin husband to a furniture store and bought all the furniture we needed to move in. So, after a couple of weeks, we moved from the Chelsea hotel to the Alameda Apartments. Our life in New York had just begun on a more permanent basis.

The next objective I had was to find Katy a job and also to enroll her in the city's university system. Katy was not sure what he wanted to major in. She thought about accounting or teaching. But she enrolled at the Baruch College, which was basically the liberal arts branch of the city university system. She started taking some courses in Accounting and English. In addition, she was able to get a job as a sales lady in Korvette, a clothing store on 5th Avenue in Manhattan. It was not easy, as she had to be on her feet all day. So, I knew that at some point she needed to find something better. What about Grolier, I thought!

I had been with Grolier a few months already and they transferred me to their executive floor to work for Ms. Ida Kelly who managed their keypunch operations from the 12th floor. This floor also had the offices of the President, Vice President and all the directors. I became very good friend with Ms Kelly. She was really Italian but married to an Irishman but her make up was all Latin. Very nervous but efficient and I became her confidant on all issues regarding the company. So, one day I asked her how to get a job for my girlfriend there. She told me what to do and before long Katy became an employee of Grolier as well. This was the beginning of a long list of relatives that ultimately went to work for Grolier, including my mother, my future mother-in-law Aida, my uncle Miguel who had just arrived from Cuba but knew the language, my other uncle Eduardo who worked in their accounting department, Katy's aunt Silvia who went to work for the Howell Book House a company that Grolier's president owned to publish dog books. And to think that the only one who had to pay an employment agency to get this job was me!

In the meantime, I continued with my college studies. Katy was doing the same thing after work and life moved on. I started to get anxious about working for a publishing company while studying engineering. I really wanted to change jobs to a company more in line with my studies. But, God works in mysterious ways – a relative of the family was an engineer with Con Edison, the electric company of New York City and one day he told me to give him a resume that he would submit it to their employment office. Before long I had an interview in their Distribution Engineering group and was hired as a technician. I became a member of 4-man team – the Assistant Engineer in charge of the team, Harold Lane, his assistant Ed Latham and the two technicians, Sal Vetere and myself. Our job was to identify potential overloads due to new businesses in one section of the borough of Brooklyn and then prepare a work order to install new transformers on those areas. All of the technicians working on that floor were doing the same thing – going to college at night to get their engineering degree. Con Ed was very flexible with us, especially during exams time. I enjoyed my time with Con Ed and made very good friends there. The year was 1962.

Life was moving right along. My father had found a job in a large pharmacy in Brooklyn. My mother was working at Grolier in their correspondence department. My sister Olga was in high school in Queens, Katy was working at Grolier also in their correspondence department. And I was busy with my new job at Con Ed and school.

One day in October, while still working at Grolier and just before starting my new job at Con Edison, I received a call from my mom that my father was taken to the hospital. It was a very cold morning and while he was waiting for the pharmacy to open he started to feel chest pains and was rushed to the hospital. It was never very clear whether he had a heart attack. It never bothered him again but it was very traumatic for me. My dad was 54 years old. However, he recovered well and went back to work within a few days. It is interesting how you never think about death until something like this happens. On that day, I became aware of my parents' mortality and what it meant to me. I was growing up very fast and this just added more maturity to my character.

Katy was starting to make plans to bring her parents out of Cuba. This would be a major undertaking given the situation there. They would have to leave through either Spain or Mexico. It would not be easy or cheap but it was our new mission and we were going to make it happen!

Katy's life with her aunt Lucy was very interesting. Her aunt was one of those movie characters that you never forget the moment you meet her. One day, as we were returning to her apartment we saw her sitting on the steps and wondered what was happening. She had fallen on the sidewalk and appeared to have broken her ankle. We decided to take her to the hospital but she only wanted to go to Bellevue Hospital because "they had the best doctors." Once in the hospital we had to go through the admission process. She needed me to be her translator. During the interview the lady asked her how old she was and before I was able to answer she replied in English "53" as if by doing so, no one else would know it! She checked into the hospital where she stayed over a week or so. During that time Katy stayed at our house so she would not have to stay in the apartment by herself. Finally, Lucy was released and she started her own therapy at her house with my help. She was afraid to let go of her crutches so one night I told her it was time to do so. We removed her crutches and she slowly started to walk by herself and was fine after that. She never had any other problems and lived to be 99 years of age!!

Soon, we started to discuss getting married. We felt we both had jobs and could support ourselves. So, after some discussion we decided to get married in July 1964. We chose July 4, which was, not only a Saturday but also my dad's birthday and we thought he would be very happy to see us get married on his birthday. Of course, Katy's parents were still in Cuba and there was a strong likelihood that they would not be present for our wedding. But, we felt it was important to get married now and not wait any longer. We were very matured for our ages – Katy was 19 and I was 20. So, we set the date, Saturday, July 4, 1964. We picked the church at St. Francis Xavier High School, a Jesuit school on 17th Street and 7th Avenue. So, prior to the religious ceremony we had to get married in the court of law. Since I was 20 I needed my parents to sign for me since at that time, men were only adults in New York at the age of 21 but women at 18.

Our Wedding Day – July 4, 1964, New York City

The wedding went well. Katy's uncle Tony, took her down the aisle. Our reception party was held at the Nacional, a Spanish social club on 14th Street that Katy's uncle belonged to. We had over 100 people in the reception mostly family and very close friends. We could not afford a big party since our income was small and we needed our savings to buy furniture for our apartment. A few weeks before our wedding we bought just about every piece of furniture we needed, mostly in stores down in Delancey Street, which was famous for stores with good quality products at reasonable prices.

Our first night was spent at a Howard Johnson on Eight Street and 52nd Avenue in Manhattan. We borrowed my dad's car and left the next day for Washington, D.C. We wanted to spend time there and see the museums but most importantly, President Kennedy's tomb at Arlington Cemetery. President Kennedy was killed back on November 22, 1963 and we remembered vividly those few days when, while watching the arrangement of Lee Harvey Oswald, we saw Jack Ruby shoot him right on national television. Those were very difficult days. The whole country felt this loss. We were not big fans of the president since we felt he had let down the Cuban community during both the Bay of Pigs invasion and then later on during the Cuban Missile crisis. Both times the president had an opportunity to get rid of Castro and communism in Cuba, a country just 90 miles away from the U.S. mainland and he failed to do so. Nevertheless, we felt badly that a young man with a young family had lost his life. Perhaps if he had taken stronger action in Cuba, his life might have been spared. Only God knows!

Back in D.C. we visited his tomb at Arlington Cemetery, which was still in the original state with a small white picket fence around a flame. We also visited some of the museums and after a few days, left DC and drove south. Our plan was to visit Katy's cousin Lourdes who lived in Southern Pines,

N.C. with her husband and 3 children at the time. On our way down we stopped in a store in Virginia and bought a whole Virginia ham to bring as a present. We stayed in a small motel in Southern Pines and bought all of our cooking utensils in that town! After a few days, we returned to New York and our new apartment at the Alameda building. My parents had prepared a welcome back party with friends and relatives and our life took a new turn.

Finally in 1965, after a lot of letters to the Mexican government, Katy's parents were allowed to leave Cuba on a temporary basis for Mexico City. They moved into an apartment house that was primarily housing for students of the university and we paid for all their expenses during the three months they lived in Mexico. Eventually, they were given permission to come to the U.S. and arrive in New York in October 1965. They moved in with us and started the process of assimilating the new culture while looking for work. My father-in-law, who was a school teacher and pharmacist in Cuba was able to find a job at a pharmaceutical manufacturing plant in Queens and my mother-in-law also found a position at Grolier Enterprises where she joined the rest of the family who already worked there. Life started again to become more stable. I was working at Con Edison and going to school at night and Katy was still working at Grolier. Our goal was to find a way to complete my college education as rapidly as possible so, having children would have to wait until I was done.

Sometimes, we do not appreciate the good things life has to offer until it is too late. The Alameda building provided us with the comfort of family. There were many family members living there. Our holiday celebrations were done together at someone's apartment and we had a lot of fun. We had made some changes in our finances that enabled me to go to school full time while Katy found a better paying job.

One day we received news that my maternal grandfather Eduardo had passed away in Cuba at the age of 85. This was devastating for the family and I took it very hard since I was very close to him. On top of that, the month before, we received news that Katy's cousin, Marylo, had died from a diabetic coma. Both events were very sad and it was hard to deal with them. But what I did not know was that my dad was also dying of lung cancer! He had been interned at Columbus Hospital complaining of shortness of breath. Without our knowledge he had been to a private physician who diagnosed his lung cancer but he did not want us to know. Eventually, three weeks later he was dead. They had performed a biopsy at Columbus hospital where he was and did not yield any positive signs of cancer but the doctor who was treating him at the hospital assured me that my dad was dying of cancer. There was no time for surgery and one early Sunday morning on April 2, 1967 at the age of 58 he passed away. This was the first time I had faced a catastrophic event as losing one's parent is. I was in the middle of midterm exams and had to deal with my dad's passing and all the arrangements for his funeral while still studying to pass my exams. A very difficult period of time but experiences that shaped our character and gave us time to reflect how precious life was and how important it was to appreciate what God has given us and live the present as it is meant to be – a gift from God!

Resuming college during the day division was critical. It would enable me to complete my Electrical Engineering degree in two more years instead of four at night. My in-laws were very supportive and helpful both financially and otherwise. I do not think I could have done it without their help. Planning for a family was still out of the question. We could wait and do it later after I had a professional job with a much better salary. This was the plan. It was the Spring of 1967. My mom was in mourning with both the death of her dad as well as my dad. But, given her strong spirit she made the best of it. This was also a good inspiration to me.

Someone once said, show me your plans and I will show you God laughing. See, one of the things we are taught in catholic school is that God really controls our life. He is the reason we are in this world and he is the Master Planner. Things always go better when we allow Him to handle our life. It is when we think we know better that things go wrong.

One Sunday afternoon, while having a nice late lunch at home, the four of us (my in-laws and us), Katy suddenly complained that she was very light headed and immediately fainted. What a shock for all. We thought she had died. I ran out of the apartment to find a doctor friend who lived in another part of the building. My father-in-law ran to another apartment and rushed in to let everyone know that Katy had died! It was pandemonium! Fortunately by the time we both got back she had regained consciousness. We were still perplexed as to what had happened and when we asked other family members they recommended we go see an obstetrician. We called a very good friend of mine and they recommended their obstetrician, Dr. Magin Sagarra, an excellent doctor who was Cuban and had completed his medical studies at the Sorbonne in Paris, France.

The following week we paid Dr. Sagarra a visit and after his examination he came back and said: "Have you ever seen in the movies where the wife faints and everyone is happy because she is pregnant"? Well, your wife is expecting!! I was very surprised at first given that we had already embarked on my remaining two years in college during the day without a job. But, I quickly reacted and became very, very happy. We were going to have a child, our first child!! We felt that God would not abandon us. I would go and get a job after school and perhaps a small student loan and move on.

Our son was born on October 3, 1967, after more than 24 hours of labor at Doctors Hospital in Manhattan. A very healthy boy who was always hungry and slept well at night. The perfect baby for someone who was studying all the time. I could not believe I had a son. If only my dad was alive to see it, but I'm sure he was watching the whole thing from heaven.

Our children: Henry Luis and Mary Jean. May 1971, New Jersey

Luckily, I was able to find a job at Howell Book House, the publishers of many dog books, thanks to Silvia, Katy's aunt who was working there. I went to City Bank and took a $1500 educational loan and with help from my father-in-law we made ends meet. It was tough but I was determined to make it. Eventually, in June 1968 I finally graduated as an Electrical Engineer from The City College of New York. I was extremely proud of having accomplished that major milestone and knew that good things would happen in the future.

Our children: Henry Luis and Mary Jean. May 1971, New Jersey

My Professional Life

I started my professional career back with Con Edison as an engineer in their cadet program. This program consisted of a two-year training in different parts of the company. My first assignment was working in the Electrical Engineering department of the Ravenswood Generating Station in Queens, New York. This was one of the largest generating stations in the system and I learned many facets of how to generate electricity, how to start and shutdown a generating station and so forth. It was very interesting and met many good friends, one of which later became Con Edison's Chief Executive Officer.

In the meantime, Katy became pregnant with our second child. In November of 1968, the electrical union called for a general strike and we, members of management, were asked to replace all union members throughout the Con Ed system. I was assigned at a substation in lower Manhattan which was underground and spent two weeks there keeping the electricity flowing along with other colleagues. The strike was settled just before Thanksgiving. The new year brought our next born. Mary Jean was born in January 12, 1969. When Katy started to have contractions we called Dr. Sagarra and he told us to take her to the hospital. It was late at night and the streets were full of snow from a recent storm. There was a car double parked next to mine so the only way I could get out of that spot was to drive my car on to the sidewalk. Our small VW beetle performed well and we eventually arrived at the hospital. Again, as her brother before her, she was born at

Doctors Hospital with Dr. Sagarra, the attending physician. She was a small baby but very cute. Her eyes were wide open. We were all very happy. This time things were not as bad as before, since we were able to manage it better.

My career with Con Edison continue well. After the first assignment in Ravenswood, I moved on to another department back in headquarters at 4 Irving Place in Manhattan. One of my mentors at Con Edison was now a Vice President and he kept tabs on my progress. However, I found life at Con Edison moved very slowly. There was little room for innovation as every aspect of the company was set. The top management were people who had grown up in that system and had little desire to make any changes. It was like working for a government agency. So, during one of our vacation trips to Florida, I talked with a friend of mine who was also in the family and working at RCA Computer Systems Division and he arranged an interview with his department head. RCA had their big computer division at that plant and was growing fast. This was an opportunity to show my intellect in a technical area that I would enjoy. The only hurdle was to pass the interview and get an offer of employment.

One day, we drove from our apartment in Miami Beach where we were vacationing to Palm Beach Gardens. It was a very rainy day and we stayed at a Holiday Inn in Singer Island. The next day I went for my interview. One of the engineers sat with me and gave me an exam. Most of what he tested me on were areas that I knew from my college days in electrical engineering and I aced the test. Afterwards, I met with the head of the group and he was very impressed with the test and told me that he thought I would be getting an offer. Needless to say, I was very happy with the outcome and as we drove back to Miami, we started to discuss plans for moving. A couple of days later the office at the rental apartment where we were staying in Miami Beach called me with a telegram. The offer had arrived and I was to contact RCA personnel to make arrangements for moving and to look around for a place to live. As soon as we arrived back in Queens we started to make arrangements to vacate the apartment and move. Eventually we arrived in Palm Beach Gardens, found a small house to rent in North Palm Beach and started my new job.

The job was very challenging. I was part of the Design and Development group. Our department was broken into two team – a digital team and analog team. I was placed in the analog team responsible for developing a universal oscillator network for RCA's Spectra mainframe computers. Imagine those big, refrigerator size computers which today you can fit in a laptop with 10x more capabilities. However, in the home front things were not working out as well. The area that we had moved in was primarily retired people and they did not appreciate little kids running around the sidewalks. Also, our house was small and we had left Katy's parents back in New York after living with us since they arrived from Cuba. My mother was also in New York. The bottom line was that we missed our old environment and families. It was time to move back!

This was a difficult thing for me to do since just four months before RCA had moved us to Florida and now I was to tell them that we needed to go back. So, before I went to talk to my manager I started working with a headhunter who found me an interview with Lockheed in Plainfield, New Jersey. With that in hand I went to see my manager and explained to him our decision. He tried to talk me out of it but when he realized I was determined to leave he said not to follow up with the Lockheed interview and to give him a couple of days to arrange for some interviews with RCA in New Jersey.

So, right after Thanksgiving 1969 I flew to Philadelphia and interviewed with RCA in Cherry Hill, N.J. and also in Somerville. N.J. The interview in Cherry Hill was for a position in their new computer plant in Marlboro, Mass. Fortunately, the offer came back from Somerville, New Jersey plant that was part of the Components sector of RCA responsible for design and production of vacuum tubes and now the new digital products called COSMOS. Needless to say, I readily accepted the offer as I liked working for RCA and this new assignment appeared to be exciting and challenging. I never interviewed with Lockheed.

I started my new life with RCA in Somerville, New Jersey in January 1970. The division soon changed its name from Components to Solid State. The emphasis became more in digital devices as vacuum tubes were becoming a thing of the past. Everything was going digital and I was fortunate enough to be one of the pioneers of this new technology which RCA had discovered and was trying hard to convince everyone that this was the new evolution of digital technology with many inherent benefits over the other ones. It took a while but eventually everyone jumped on the bandwagon and today it is the only digital technology used in all products, CMOS.

In parallel to that we found an apartment in Roselle, NJ where we could all live together again and was close enough to the bus stop where Katy's parents could ride to their jobs in Manhattan. This apartment was very small and we were very crowded but we wanted to save to buy a house as soon as possible and, eventually after a little over a year, with my in-laws help we bought a bi-level house in Linden, New Jersey, also a block away from the bus stop. It was a nice house with a large patio for the kids to play. We were finally settled and ready for our next chapter in life. The kids were growing and attending elementary school and Katy had decided to go back to college and get her teaching degree from Kean College. I was thrilled when she finally enrolled back in college.

I knew she always wanted to finish her college degree and be a professional and since our children were now in school full time, she was able to do so without interference. I also decided to get my Master Degree. Initially, I enrolled at Stevens Institute of Technology in an Engineering Management program but later decided to change to Rutgers University in New Brunswick, which was a few miles from RCA in Somerville and I could stop there on my way home. I enrolled in the Master Degree in Electrical Engineering program and in 1974 received my degree.

Studying for my master's degree was not easy. Those were the days of high unemployment, the oil embargo and RCA was laying off engineers every week. Every day when I left for Rutgers in the afternoon I considered myself lucky that I had made it through another day at RCA. However, after a while I decided I was just going to concentrate in doing the best job I could and to study hard for my school program and let God decide the rest. So, I made it through those difficult times.

My first job in Somerville was in the Applications Engineering department. This was the group that resolved technical issues with our customers and also wrote all the technical data sheets for our products as well as application notes explaining how to use our products. We also developed a book on COSMOS technology and I was responsible for a few chapters of that book. I became a member of a COSMOS industry standardization committee along with others companies like Fairchild, Intel, Harris, Motorola, TI, etc and we used to meet in Palo Alto, California once a quarter to develop standards for this new product line so our customers would be able to understand the product's data sheets regardless of which company was developing it. It made it easier for everyone. There were a lot of key people represented in this committee that later on became "giants" in the semiconductor industry in California.

But just when you think everything is under control, God decided to make His presence felt. One day I received a call that my mother had gone for a check up and the doctor had found cancer on her uterus. My mother was 56 years old and very strong and healthy and this shocked all of us. Our new saga was about to begin. Soon thereafter they operated on her and did a total hysterectomy to get rid of any signs of cancer. I remember seeing the doctor at the hospital right after the operation who told me, "today I saved your mom's life." I was very happy and believed him. However, a year later she started to complain about pressure on her lower abdomen. When she went to see the doctor he felt it was better if she went to Sloan Kettering Memorial Hospital to get another opinion. The doctors at Memorial decided to do an exploratory surgery to determine what they had to deal with and found that the cancer had spread and they were not able to do radiation treatment but try chemotherapy instead. The doctors at Memorial felt that the original surgery had not gone deep enough to remove all cancer cells and now they had spread. So, my mother started her ordeal, which she bore valiantly for the next year and in October 4, 1976 she passed away during the early morning hours. I was not there with her during her last moments, as we did not know she was so close to death. We had visited her the day before where she filled up a birthday card for my son and she was in good spirits. It was the worst moment of my life. I had to cling to all of my Christian beliefs. Katy was a big help during these trying days. My mom, the eternal optimist was now in heaven. She had finally rested but we were left with a big void that, even to this date, it had never been filled! I missed my mother every day!

So, my life with RCA in Somerville moved on and I spent time in their design group, marketing team and eventually became manager of the Applications Engineering group until my transfer to Palm Beach Gardens, Florida. Interesting that we were going back to Florida after eight years in New Jersey!

How this did happen? Well, one day while I was still applications engineering manager, the vice president of engineering and his twin brother, my boss, asked me to go to lunch with them. During lunch they told me they wanted to make some changes and wanted me to move to a new job called systems engineering. This new job had no staff, no mission, and no budget. The other choice was to fill a vacancy in the Palm Beach Gardens facility as chief engineer.

A note about Palm Beach Gardens – after I transferred to Somerville in 1970, this facility which was manufacturing RCA Spectra 70 mainframe computers, was shut down. The shut down happened in 1971 when RCA Board of Directors realized they were not going to take over leadership of computers from IBM. They were running a huge debt and making very little progress against IBM. So, they took a $500M write-off and sold their products to Sperry Univac. In the meantime, the Solid State Division was expanding into a finer geometry technology and needed new space so they decided to move their new group into the "old" computer facility in Palm Beach Gardens. A new group started in the plant to manufacture LSI (Large Scale Integration) devices and was looking for people to staff it. The plant manager, who I had a lot of confrontations with, especially when he wanted to ship products that had not passed all the reliability and quality requirements, was now asking for me to fill the vacancy of chief engineer.

So, given the choices, I discussed it with Katy and we decided to take the Florida job. We felt the children were now older, well into their elementary school. We were also older and more experienced. The only issue was Katy's parents but we felt we could eventually work that out. Katy could transfer to FAU to finish her teaching degree. But, I think the hand of God was there guiding us. He was the final decision maker. So, we moved back to Palm Beach Gardens to start my new job in the old RCA facility.

RCA took care of our house in Linden. They bought our house and set up us with a realtor in Palm Beach Gardens to help us find a house there. Eventually, we bought an existing house in Palm Beach Gardens very close to all schools and the plant. It was much bigger than what we had in Linden and in May 1978, we moved back to Florida.

The children continued their elementary schooling, Katy transferred her credits to FAU and continued with her teaching degree and I started my new job at the plant. RCA's goal was to make this facility their new state-of-the-art semiconductor plant where the newest technology would be built. We were now in the LSI (Large Scale Integration) environment trying to build products with much finer geometry. We were expanding and hiring.

It took a while to get used to the new area. Everyone missed the family and our friends up north. We did not miss the weather but it took time to get used to the much warmer climate but eventually we adapted well. The kids were happy and started to make new friends. Our street was loaded with kids so that made the transition much easier and faster for them. Most of our friends and Florida family were in the Miami area but through the kids' school we started to make new friends.

I had many new challenges in my new job. A new group that needed some restructuring. However, I was happy and still part of the same company so the transition was smooth. In addition I was asked to be the Palm Beach Gardens rep at all monthly operation review back in Somerville, NJ. This was good as I was able to stay in touch with my colleagues up north while keeping tabs on my in-laws who had stayed in New York. Our goal was to eventually move them to Florida to be close to us.

Katy graduated from FAU with her Bachelors of Arts in Education in December 1980 and soon thereafter, started working in some of the high schools in the area, among them Rosarian Academy, Santaluces High School and eventually, Palm Beach Gardens High School – only 3 blocks from our house! She finally did it and I was very, very proud of her. I was also very happy that her long dream of getting a college degree had come true thanks to her hard work and perseverance.

The children finished their primary schooling and moved on to Howell Watkins Middle School and then on to Palm Beach Gardens High School. They made new friends and am pleased to say that they were always smart in the friends they picked. Katy and I were very proud of their good judgment and commitment to doing well in school. We always told them that they had to work hard to enjoy a professional life and not to depend on anyone.

RCA continue to expand with new people at headquarters in Somerville as well as in our plant in Florida. Until one day in 1985 – our son Henry was just starting at the University of Miami. We were called to the cafeteria for a major announcement: RCA was shutting down Palm Beach Gardens. I was already aware of this decision because of the plant's inability to print finer geometries due to vibration from the trains passing east of the plant every day. Every time the train went by we were unable to print our wafers so this basically put a stop to RCA's goals of making Palm Beach Gardens their state-of-the-art facility. A wafer is a thin slice of semiconductor material, such as silicon crystal, used in the fabrication of integrated circuits and other microdevices.

The announcement established a complete shut down date of December 1986. There were job opportunities in Somerville as well as in our sister facility in Findlay, Ohio. I was fortunate to get a commitment from my old boss in Somerville to join his group as a Program Manager. While I was thankful for this trust, I, nevertheless, wanted to stay in Florida. I did not want to go back. So, I sent out over 50 resumes to see what would happen with my eyes set on either Martin Marietta in Orlando or Harris Semiconductor in Melbourne.

I was very hopeful that I would be able to stay in Florida. I knew it was the right thing to do. Again, I prayed and asked God to help me find a suitable job that would be the least disruptive to the family. One day in November 1985 I received a call from Martin Marietta to come up and interview for a position in their VLSI Microelectronics Center in Orlando, Florida. They also asked me to bring Katy so she could look at real estate while I was doing the interview. This was what I was waiting for. It looked like I was going to get the job. The interview was good. I liked the people I talked to and was very impressed by the work they were doing in semiconductors, my area of expertise. Katy was able to look at some houses but nothing firm yet.

We returned home just before Thanksgiving and were told by Martin's Personnel department that nothing was going to happen until early the following year. The company was going on their Christmas vacations and most of their managements were leaving as well. I did not mind. I felt I had the job and started to make plans to leave RCA.

However, one day in January 1986 the head of personnel at Martin called me to tell me that they had decided to extend an offer to a former employee who wanted to return. I was devastated but not defeated.

On January 28, 1986 while I was having a meeting with a major defense contractor in our plant, we heard about the Challenger explosion. We went outside in the patio and saw the smoke traces of the disaster in the sky. Soon, thereafter, I went to my office and called the gentleman that interviewed me at Martin to find out why the offer had been withdrawn but, more importantly, to let him know I was still very interested to work for Martin Marietta. He appreciated my call. He told me that it was a decision made at the Vice Presidential level and he did not want to get in the middle of it but that he would keep my resume on his desk for the next opportunity. He liked my credentials and character and wanted to find a way to get me on board. Did he really mean this or was it the political thing to say? I thought he was sincere.

I continue to look for other job opportunities in Florida until one day in March 1986 when Katy and I were getting ready to fly to Spain with a group of her students, I received a phone call from that same gentleman who had promised to keep my resume on his desk, to let me know he wanted me to come back for an interview. The person they had hired earlier was not working out and he felt I would be a much better fit for the position. So, after our trip to Spain, I went back, interviewed with a few individuals and was offered the job. Needless to say, how happy we were with this change in our lives. I was able to stay in Florida with a very good company and least disruptive to the family.

My time at Martin was very gratifying. I developed a very good relationship with my team as well as with supervision. My new position was Manager of Wafer Fabrication for the Microelectronics Center, responsible for all semiconductor fabrication operations in support of Martin's key programs.

It was called in "high tech" jargon VHSIC Fab Operations that stood for Very High Scale Integrated Circuit fabrication. Our role was to take all new designs and turn them into integrated circuits ready to be installed in all key products. It was very high scale because of the fine geometry utilized to get as much circuitry into same piece of silicon wafer. Martin felt they could not get any of the major semiconductor houses interested in their requirements due to their low volume so having an in-house capability made sense. I had a team of highly experienced semiconductor specialists and our success rate was very high.

However, all good things eventually come to an end. The end happened in 1988 when I presented a capital reinvestment plan to our upper management. I tried to explain to them that when you are in the semiconductor business you must replenish your capital investment to the tune of 10% of your invested capital. They were surprised, especially when they had pieces of equipment in their factories that have been working over the last 20 years, so they decided it was too big of an investment for them to continue to pursue and decided to return to the open market to get their requirement served by the semiconductor industry. My immediate concern was to find jobs for all of our people, either inside Martin or in other semiconductor companies. I was concerned about my future but did not let that interfere with my responsibility. I contacted a lot of people and eventually we were able to place about 90% of our team.

Fortunately, I was asked to stay with the company and temporarily worked in a small shop supporting all wiring operations for key programs. Ultimately I was permanently assigned to the Electrical Engineering department responsible for Components Engineering. I was fortunate to work for a great individual. Very caring and extremely smart. My job was easier because of him. There were many interesting programs at Martin. I had a "secret" security clearance, which enabled me to spend time in various classified programs in support of the U.S. Department of Defense activities. In addition to my responsibilities of the Components Engineering department I was also responsible for supporting the different programs throughout Orlando. This support was provided with key engineers that were experts in different fields – from radar, semiconductor, and antenna technologies among others. Basically we provided the electrical engineering support for Martin's Orlando programs.

At this time, the cold war appeared to be coming to an end. Presidents Reagan and later Bush had "convinced" the Soviets that they would be better if they eliminated communism. This also created a major reduction of military programs, which affected our company so layoffs began. I spent a major part of my time defining which engineers were needed or not throughout the system. Any engineer that we were unable to find a position became available for layoffs. There was a very precise process that we had to go through based on the Human Resources guidelines to make sure it was equitable and fair.

Around this time, I received a call from Motorola to come down to Boynton Beach and interview for a position in their Paging Division. Given the situation at Martin and the fact that I was no longer enjoying myself, I decided to proceed with the interview. It was June 1990.

The interview was very interesting. The person that interviewed me for a position as TOP (Technical Operations

Manager) was the son of a former professor at my old high school, Colegio Baldor in Havana, Cuba and when he found out I had been to Baldor, our conversation turned to those school years in Havana. Later on in another interview he brought me a copy of Baldor's yearbook with my picture in it.

The author and wife celebrating their 25th wedding anniversary in Siesta Key, FL

I was very impressed with the work environment at Motorola. There were a lot of young people working very hard to make new pagers. It was very invigorating and I felt I could make a good contribution there. But, I did not really want to leave Martin. I did not want to leave our neighborhood in Tuscawilla. Katy had a good job at Lake Mary High School, which she loved, and Mary Jean had just started at UCF, a driving distance from the house. If I accepted the job, it would mean a lot of changes and disruptions to our lives once again. We had been in the Orlando area for a mere 4 years, had a good social network, and were considered a fast tracker at Martin and another change was really very undesirable. But, again, God works in mysterious ways!

I called Motorola with the intention of rejecting the job but they kept insisting. They told me they would provide me with a nice sign-on-bonus. They would make up any difference between the selling price of my house vs. market value, which would amount to about $47K. The final hurdle was that I would want to stay at Martin until November 16, 1990 in order to become vested which would represent a small retirement check at 65. So, they again, told me that would be fine. To go ahead and accept the job right away in September and report to work in December. Basically, every time I provided an excuse not to accept the job, they would remove that obstacle.

Katy and I discussed it further and we felt that God wanted me to take the job and so I did. A new corporate adventure was about to begin!

Motorola was a different type of company. There were a lot of projects going on at the same time. The Paging Division was growing very fast. We were hiring. Sales were breaking new records. My position at first was to manage all the technical resources in support of our Boynton Beach manufacturing operations. My official title was TOP (Technical Operations) Manager.

I found Motorola to be a very exciting company. The division was chartered to design and manufacture all paging products sold under the Motorola logo. We had feeder facilities around the world, primarily in Puerto Rico and Singapore. My team was responsible for supporting all manufacturing engineering activities in Boynton Beach, Florida. This included manufacturing, testing and product return evaluations. We also had responsibility for coordinating with the design teams in the development of new products in the model shop area.

During the fall of 1992, soon after the infamous Hurricane Andrews, I was asked by management to take over our Puerto Rico facilities to resolve many personnel issues that were taken place there. Originally, this was supposed to be a temporary assignment but after getting involved in all the issues, they offered me the position of VP and General Manager of all operations, a job I eagerly accepted since it was challenging and very rewarding. I found the people there very productive and with their long Motorola tradition, willing to do what it took to help improve the reputation and productivity of the plant. We embarked in a very aggressive mission of resolving all personnel issues which required some terminations and replacements of key jobs, increase overall production and improve the overall quality level at the facility.

The Puerto Rico facility was located in Vega Baja. Motorola had leased three building from the government. I was excited to take over this plant in a Spanish-speaking country. It brought me back to my own culture and I enjoyed every minute of that assignment. In addition to Pagers, the facilities manufactured batteries for radio phones and small portable infrastructure computers in support of public radio phones. The labor force was dedicated, friendly, and hard-working. They all wanted to prove to the rest of Motorola that Puerto Rico could be as good as any of the other plants in the system. We accomplished a lot during this time and I will always remembered those days of my professional life fondly.

In the spring of 1993, due to some management changes in Boynton Beach, I was asked to come back to Boynton and take over all manufacturing operations there. This was a promotion for me that was hard to refuse. I still had responsibilities for the Puerto Rico operations. In May of 1993 I returned to Boynton Beach. Katy and I missed our short time there very much and came back with a gratifying feeling of our time in the island.

My move to Boynton was not without challenges! As I had learned many times before, you have to adapt to changes, especially when a company is growing as fast as Motorola was growing. To my surprised, the job I was coming to fill had been promised by my predecessor to two other individuals who were now reporting to me! Interesting dilemma that I faced on my return. I kept asking myself – why did I give up such a fulfilling job in Puerto Rico to come to this political hornet's nest?

After some discussions, we came to the understanding that I was their supervisor and it would be better for everyone to try to work together to meet the challenges we were being paid to handle. Ultimately, both persons left the organization. One to move to Singapore to get overseas experience and the other to our sister facility in Plantation, Florida. The changes were not easy but they had to be done for the betterment of the whole organization and Motorola.

I spent 3 years in this new assignment and after 4 short years with the company, I became a Vice President and Director of Motorola. This new recognition moved me into the executive ranks of Paging with all the benefits associated with the new title. I was very happy and felt I had made the right move to come to Motorola. As part of my new perks, I was entitled to a company car. I always wanted to have a Cadillac and most of my other VP colleagues were getting Cadillacs, so I did same thing. How many people can say that in 4 years you had a job that was rewarding, exciting, challenging and well recognized? The company continued to expand in pagers. We were now manufacturing both one-way and two-way pagers. Our two-way operations was moved to Ft. Worth, Texas and many of our colleagues moved there with it. The Ft. Worth operations had an engineering team that reported to me so I got to spend a lot of time in Ft. Worth. Eventually, management offered me a position there, responsible for all infrastructure support for the new paging technology. This was a very difficult decision!

I remember when I was offered that new job. We were in Beijing, China, attending a TME (Team for Manufacturing Excellence) meeting. These meetings were held once every quarter at different locations throughout the world and I was the chairperson of that committee. One of the benefits of working for Motorola was the fact that we traveled the world to many of our sister facilities, among them, Dublin, Singapore, Puerto Rico, Beijing, China, Scotland, etc. Katy was able to accompany me on many of these trips. On our way to China, while changing planes at the Dallas-Ft. Worth airport, I received a page to call my old boss who was now working in the Ft. Worth plant. He wanted to let me know that everyone wanted me to take the position and move to Ft. Worth. It was a promotion, which meant more money and a clear path to become Corporate VP. Katy, who was with me on our way to Beijing, was a great source of support, as always, to let me see the pros and cons of the move. But, at the end, it would be my decision. My old boss told me that our Sr. VP in charge of Paging would be talking to me about it in Beijing. Needless to say, I had a very long trip with a lot of concerns. Finally, after we arrived a day later, I had my meeting and now understood very well what the position would be. I wrestled with it for another day or two and then made my decision. I would not take the job in Texas.

Throughout my career, I have always put my family's wellbeing ahead of my job. While this position was an advancement, it would put undo stress on the family. True, the job was challenging but the negatives outweigh the positives and I turned it down. Senior management was not happy with that but I did what I felt was best for the family. A few years later, that whole operation shut down and many of those folks found themselves without a career. So, I guess, again, God worked his divine intervention and helped me make the right call.

Motorola Paging continued to grow at gigantic steps. Both, one-way and two-way paging were a big success in the marketplace. We were building new facilities all over the world with the latest being the Chihuahua plant in northern Mexico. This would be a brand new plant to build pagers and offset some of the load from the Puerto Rico facilities. Puerto Rico was going through some political changes that we felt may jeopardize the financial benefits we were receiving and it may require some fundamental changes in our long-term strategy.

Our decision to build a plant in Chihuahua was a very complex one. We knew we wanted to locate in Mexico. It was close to the United States. It had a good labor pool of experienced workers. We already had experiences with some operations there. It was a good market for pagers and also close to the rest of the Latin American market. A few of us were assigned the job of picking the right location. We visited many different regions of Mexico, including Guadalajara, Aguascalientes, Monterrey, Leon, and Chihuahua. All the governors involved in those regions presented their best plan and Chihuahua won by a big margin. So, we built a state-of-the-art facility there and used some of the associates from our Puerto Rico facilities to help train their Mexican counterparts. We had enough business to keep both facilities going. With Chihuahua, we already had facilities in Dublin, Ireland, Tianjin, China, Puerto Rico, and Singapore.

The global economy was changing and wireless phones were becoming cheaper with more capabilities. There was a dark cloud on the horizon!

Around this time, Paging went through some changes and after being associated with manufacturing for a while, I wanted to run a business. I wanted to move from Operations to New Business in order to gain some exposure and help my future growth with Motorola. So, in 1996, I moved from manufacturing to Derivatives Technologies Division (DTD) as head of their worldwide sales and marketing team. This new organization was chartered to develop new applications using paging technology. It was new and challenging and I felt this was the right move for me. What I really wanted was to be a general manager of the Paging Latin America Division but the job was not available, so I settled for DTD.

One of the projects we embarked upon was to build a phone into a Palm Pilot PDA. It would have been the first "smart phone" in the world, but our senior management turned it down. To this day, I still think that decision was very narrow-minded and it prevented Motorola from continuing to be the leaders in cellular technology. At that time, our competition was Nokia and not Apple!

The paging demand continued to decrease as more people turned to cellular phones. Their prices were coming down and you could have more features than those found on a pager. We started to look for ways to shut down some of our facilities or lease them to cellular. With this situation, I was promoted to General Manager of the One-Way DTD. The two-way DTD was based in Ft. Worth where the rest of the two-way paging operations resided. But it was not long when our business plan was cut back and my position was no longer secured. I needed to find another position within Motorola.

A major reorganization at the Corporate level, had created a new sector, called Integrated Electronics Systems Sector (IESS). The role of this new organization was to adapt Motorola's technologies in a variety of industrial application. It included our Automotive Telematics (On-Star) application as well as many products for the automotive industry such as sensors, fuel ignition controllers, etc. Our major customers were GM, Chrysler and Ford. We were also working with Toyota and Honda as well.

As part of their new vision, IESS wanted to have representation by regions around the world. Hence the Latin America region was created under my direction. This was the first time Motorola would try to expand their non cellular business in that region. The task was very challenging. I had to start by finding the right talent in the major markets as well as developing a business and strategic plan for the region. Our main focus would be in automotive components and navigation systems built into the car. Up to this time, all of Motorola automotive business was focused with the major auto companies in the U.S. without much regard for the needs of the Latin America region. My job was to change that and to expand our business in a way that we could address the needs of the region. This would include creating the right products for Latin America. Our main focus was with GM, Ford, Mercedes Benz and BMW.

The budget I was provided with was limited. We had to identify opportunities and then our budget would be increased. This was fair. We went to work fast. I found some key talents in Brazil and Mexico. Also, through some agreements with other Latin America divisions, I was able to share their talent in Argentina, Venezuela and Chile. We would also concentrate on Telematics (OnStar) applications as well as automotive components. The rest of the sector businesses would not be addressed at this time. We felt this was the easiest way to kick start our marketing efforts in the region by narrowing our exposure with those parts that were the most popular in Latin America.

With regards to talent, I was able to find a very capable engineer, Carlos Alberto, who had worked for GM in the U.S. and who was also Brazilian. This was a good find as he had some connections with a major automotive company and knew how that business functioned.

Our office was based in the Motorola regional headquarters in Cypress Creek, Ft. Lauderdale, Fl. I wanted Carlos Alberto to be in same office with me so we can develop the right plan and market penetration for the region. The first couple of years were going to be essential if we had any chance of expanding this market.

However, as I started to work with our engineering and marketing teams in the U.S. I realized that my mission was going to be harder than I thought. To begin with, the mindset back in Chicago and Detroit was that Latin America would never amount to anything big. This was an organization primarily focused in what they had done before and did not want to share some of their budget to help out a new area. On the other hand, the automotive companies in the region wanted to have their voices heard, independent of Detroit and felt they needed for Motorola to design products that were required for their businesses in Latin America. The bottom line was that if we wanted to succeed in Latin America we needed to have products designed and manufactured for that market. They also required that any product that we made had to be manufactured in Latin America, as close to their automotive facilities as possible.

We continued to make our case with Chicago management. We were able to start our staffing plan and hired a good sales engineer in Sao Paulo that would be responsible for developing a plan for Brazil. In addition, we hired a young engineer in Buenos Aires and Mexico City to do likewise in their respective countries. The plan was coming together and we started to have very significant meetings in those countries, primarily with automotive companies. My life became a bit hectic due to regular trips to those capitals. I spent, at least, half of my time traveling in Latin America. I became a regular at Miami International Airport and American Airlines.

9-11-2001

However, despite our best efforts, time was running out. Budgets were starting to get crunched and Motorola was going through major changes at the highest levels. One morning in September, I was traveling to Michigan via Chicago to meet with our automotive management to review plans and budgets. It was September 11, 2001. I was on an American Airlines flight from Ft. Lauderdale nonstop to Chicago and then a change to Detroit. It was a beautiful morning and there were a few other Motorolans on that flight that were traveling to Schaumburg for different reasons. Because I had a lot of miles accumulated with American I was able to upgrade to first class. The flight left on time around 8am with a scheduled arrival at 10am or so since there is an hour difference between Chicago and Florida. But the flight seemed to take a long time and after 2 hours we were still over Florida, eventually landing at O'Hare Airport in Chicago around 11:30am Chicago time. As we landed, the pilot came on the intercom to let us know that he had been asked to land and wait for further instructions. We saw hundreds of planes parked on the runway and it seemed very odd, so we got on our pagers and phones to try to find out what was going on. The pilot said he did not know what the trouble was but we needed to wait for further instructions. Almost immediately upon our arrival, a fire truck and a couple of Chicago police cars surrounded our plane and a dark haired individual seating in the coach section was forcibly removed from the plane. Our colleagues told us later that this fellow was very nervous during landing and was yelling he wanted to get out of the plane right away. After he was removed two firemen came on the plane to see if anybody was sick and needed medical attention. They also told us that we needed to wait and to forget about taking any of our personal belongings when they return to bring us to the terminal. Of course, by now we had been able to get information and found out that New York City had been attacked and the World Trade Center towers were hit by commercial airlines. I tried many times to call Katy but all circuits were busy. Finally I reached her and calmed her down. She did not know where I was and in light of what she was watching on TV, she did not know if my plane was involved. Whatever happened to that fellow the police removed from the plane we never knew but we were all sure he was involved in this terrorist plot somehow.

Finally around 12:30pm Chicago time we were allowed to disembark and were moved to some buses which took us to the terminal. Of course, we took all our carry-ons with us. The terminal was completely dark with the exception of the emergency lights. I called my office and was told the meeting in Detroit had been cancelled and that it would be best to return home. A few of the other Motorolans and I got together and decided to stay that night and then use the rental cars we had and return home very early the next day. At that moment we did not know how extensive the problem was and we decided it was prudent to stay there that night and allow the situation to unfold. We were all staying at the Hyatt Hotel in Woodfield, Illinois, not very far from the Motorola headquarters in Schaumburg.

When I checked into my room I was so anxious to turn the TV on and find out what was happening that I forgot to go to the bathroom. The next time I remembered, 3 hours had passed. I saw the total destruction of the Twin Towers, the hit on the Pentagon and the unknown situation with the flight over Pennsylvania. It was a national disaster which I could not believe it had happened! To this date, I consider myself lucky and pray for all those innocent people who died without understanding why. It was awful.

The next day, we left the hotel in three rental cars with three persons each. We would take 2-hour driving intervals and drive all the way down to Florida non-stop. We left around 5:30am and arrived home 25 hours later.

The impact of 9/11 was more than just the killing of innocent human beings. It was also a major impact on our economy and Motorola, which was already having some budgetary issues. The big driver for Motorola was the mobile phone business and competition was already eroding their market share. We were no longer able to release new products into the marketplace in time to beat competition. Many management changes were taking place and the result of all this was a major cutback at the executive levels. In addition, concerned about a future attack, we decided to put our house on the water up for sale. We signed a realtors agreement in October, 2001 and in April of 2002 we sold the house. We had already bought a new house in a new community west of us and were looking forward to the move there. We hated to sell the house on the water but it was the right thing to do. We needed to move forward!

A major announcement was made by Chris Galvin, Motorola's CEO which basically began a process of streamlining the vice presidential ranks. I was affected and soon thereafter was presented with the opportunity to take a retirement package. I was 58 years old.

It comes a time in every one's professional life that you must recognize when to fight and when to accept fate. This time I knew that if I wanted to stay with the company I would have to find a position in Chicago. My big concern was that if I chose to go to Chicago, assuming there was a position there for me, I would have to accept a lower level position and then accepting the risk of losing it at a later time without the benefits of the VP package. So, I accepted the officer's package.

The package was very liberal. It included salary for a year, assistance with employment opportunities, the company car and for those with right tenure the medical insurance. Given that I was lacking about 6 months to be entitled to the medical insurance, this became a big deal. So, working with our Human Resources team for Latin America I proposed that instead of giving me a lump sum in August of 2002, just continue to pay me monthly until February, 2003. It was same amount of money but just spread out over 6 months. I was told that it would be very difficult to get this approved and that the Executive VP for HR would have to sign it. Well, I had a good relationship with this person and as soon as he received my request, he signed it. This was a big relief for us as we would now continue to be covered with a health plan until age 65 when Medicare would take over.

So, sometimes in the Spring of 2002 I left the company for good. My official retirement became effective on February of 2003. It was hard to accept the change but, as the optimist that I am, I felt new good things would happen soon.

Afterwards, I tried to do consultant work and found a couple of opportunities through a very good friend of mine and former Motorolan to support some projects in the Caribbean for Cable & Wireless, a British telephone company. The first assignment was to identify security issues in a few islands of the Caribbean. This lasted about 2 months. The next assignment was in support of a key project for Trinidad and Tobago Telephone company. The project was related to establishing security systems in Trinidad utilizing the telephone company existing systems. Originally, I was supposed to work there half a month and the other half from home for a period of no less than six months and no more than 2 years. Unfortunately, the Trinidad and Tobago government never approved my work permit as they wanted the company to hire local talent. So, I only spent six months working from home. For those six months I was paid a very nice salary and enjoyed the research I did which to this date they are still implementing.

I also tried to start a small consulting company with 4 other colleagues from Motorola. We named this company Iter Domus and registered it with the State of Florida. Unfortunately, businesses were not spending much and we eventually phased it out.

Retirement

Upon retirement and after moving into our new house, we decided to invest part of the equity we had gained. We wanted something on the water that the family could enjoy as well. So, in 2004 we bought a condo apartment in Key Biscayne. It was expensive to maintain but it provided us with a way to have the grandkids around more often, especially the ones in Miami. They enjoyed it very much but in 2009 due to the housing bubble and with prices dropping we sold the unit.

It is interesting to note that, no matter how well you plan your life, you never really know when retirement comes. I guess it is all part of the big plan that we all come to this world with. My original plan was to retire at 65 after working for the same company all that time. Well, I retired at 58 after working for four different companies!

Now I enter a new phase of my life – dedicated husband, father and grandfather. My time is spent with friends bowling, playing cards and domino as well as with our grandkids who I help with their school work as often as they need me. I also spend time reading different books to increase my overall knowledge.

It seems that life has gone too fast. It was only yesterday that we were arriving in the U.S. and now I was retired. Much has been learned from life's experiences and in the next few paragraphs I would like to share that learning with you.

The next paragraphs are a series of experiences I have gone through in my life which I believe have given me more wisdom that I can share, because wisdom is difficult to share unless you are going through the same set of issues. Nevertheless, this is what I would like to share with you. Use it if you need to, change it if it makes sense, ignore it if it does not apply to your situation but, at least read them.

The author and his wife Katy with their oldest granchildren: Allison and Michael at Siesta Key, FL

Without becoming philosophical, how do we define life. Is it the physical duration of a person's mental and physical health or is it a combination of achievements and setbacks that prepares us for the next challenge? I would like to think of life as a combination of both issues. You cannot separate one from the other.

For us who went through a major transformation in our lives at an age when most kids are just having fun, care-free in a loving family environment with all the protection that provides, it either matures you fast or provides you with the excuse to be negative in every respect. The questions of why me God and why did this had to happen to our parents? Or why did we have to leave everything we knew, loved and were accustomed to? Those were questions that in 1960 we kept asking ourselves and our parents.

We give our parents a lot of credit. After having established a good home life with a good job or business, they found themselves with the realization that Cuba would no longer be the same and that they had to leave the country. They did not want their children to grow up in a communist state so they left. Imagine how hard that had to be! We kids thought it was tough but for them it must have been extraordinarily difficult to make that jump. Many did not speak English well enough to land a job in the U.S. right away. Most of them were in their middle 50's. They had worked hard in a country that was no longer available. So, they had no other choice but to face the unknown. They were the real heroes of this odyssey. They deserve our admiration forever and ever!!

This experience gave me courage to never allow uncertainty hold me back. I was concerned with my studies since I did not know the language but having seen what my parents were going through that gave me courage and hope. I was not afraid to tackle the unknown and I was determined to succeed no matter what.

So, my parents gave me HOPE and COURAGE!

Our pride and joy, our grandchildren in Siesta Key, Fl.
From left to right: Katie, Caroline, Allison and Michael. 2008

There was another aspect of my departure in September 1960. I was in love with the most beautiful girl in our area, Katy Mata. Leaving her was a very difficult decision which I did not want to do. I would miss her terribly without knowing when we would be together again. We were only 16 years of age but we were already making plans to be married one day once we finished our college studies. It was so difficult that during the years that we did not see each other, we would write letters every day. I was trying to work hard in school and felt that it was up to me to prepare myself and hope that one day she would leave Cuba and join me in the U.S. I used to tell my mom about my anxieties and she was also very optimistic about the whole thing. She felt that it would happen as long as I stay focused on our plans. Katy was also very optimistic in all her letters and she kept telling me that she may leave any time in the future. I believed her and this kept me going despite the hardships of separation. She set our future on those letters.

Family Picture during our 50th wedding anniversary vows renewal at St. Francis Xavier Catholic Church. June 2014

So, Katy gave me OPTIMISM and LOVE!

My early years at the Jesuit school Sagrado Corazon de Jesus, taught me how to be organized and disciplined. They gave me a Christian understanding from which I have grown to know the love of God. There were many instances where I have doubts about life after death, including heaven and hell but the Jesuits were able to ground me in a faith that came from devotion and love. The seven years I spent there were memorable. My best friends were made there as well as my future aspirations as an individual and as a member of society. Those seven years I spend with the Jesuits at an early age, provided me with a sense of responsibility to my parents, my family and God.

So, the Jesuits game me FAITH and UNDERSTANDING!

I spent over 40 years working in corporate America. It was an interesting experience over a number of different industries. From electric companies to high tech companies I learned how to adapt to many situations. I worked for good and bad managers but learned from both. I learned to temper my decisions and to surround myself with the best people money could hire. On every job I tried to always do my best. Yes, I was ambitious because I wanted a better life for my family. From my early professional years I was focused on making enough money to buy a house. With good performance and patience we accomplished that. Later on my focus was on progressing up the management ladder in order to have more influence on the people I manage. With time and patience I accomplished that. Finally in my last position I realized that time was running out and decided to make the best decision possible to preserve my family and also enjoy a comfortable retirement. And, we accomplished that. Through setbacks and moments of glory I made it. My mission was completed in total.

So, my professional life gave me KNOWLEDGE and MATURITY

So, my life has been a great ride. It has passed too fast but memorable.

I have enjoyed remembering all the facts and I hope you will enjoy reading them. The nostalgia about Cuba will always remain with me until my last day on this earth.

These are my life's lasting memories!!

Acknowledgement

There are people I need to thank in the making of this book. Their efforts on my behalf are greatly appreciated, especially my good friend Manolo Salvat of Ediciones Universal who graciously took on the job of publishing my book as well as to recommend a fine editor, Maria Cristina Zarraluqui. Maria Cristina, very patiently worked with me to insure that the right mix of information and photos was included in the book. My thanks also to Luis Garcia Fresquet for an excellent cover design.

My wife Katy who gave me very good suggestions and always encouraged me to finish it. She was instrumental in many of the chapters of the book as well as the selection of key family photos.

My children Henry Louis and Mary Jean and their spouses Doris and Kevin along with my grandchildren, Allison, Michael, Caroline and Katie who gave me the inspiration and determination of writing a book about my life story. I hope that as they read this book, they will gain a better understanding of my experiences and will be better equipped to share those with future generations.

Finally, it would be difficult to list all the people that had an impact on my life as listed on the pages of this book —my teachers, my good childhood friends, many members of my family; those professionals I worked with over the years in many fine companies.

I hope that I have been faithful and my memories reflect the life I have lived, the experiences I have shared and my belief that everything is possible if you put your mind to it and trust that the Lord will always guide you to a better path.

www.ingramcontent.com/pod-product-compliance
Lightning Source LLC
Chambersburg PA
CBHW030329080526
44584CB00012B/781